ENDORSEMENTS

The title speaks for itself: To be faithful and focused as followers of Jesus has grown increasingly difficult in our ever-changing world. Not only has the Bible come under assault from a shockingly radical segment of culture seeking to demolish any semblance of Christianity, but many churches that once held strong against these warring cultural currents have slipped from their biblical and theological moorings and gone adrift from the shoreline of orthodoxy. Thankfully, my friend and longtime board member at Dallas Seminary, Ken Horton, has provided a way back to what matters most. In *Faithful and Focused*, Ken offers a substantive but accessible heading to help steer us back on course to becoming effective and influential multipliers for Christ's kingdom. Don't shrink from digesting every word and wrestling with each motivating and thought-provoking principle in this exceptional study. Open Ken's book, learn from his experience and scholarship, embrace this fresh vision, and be changed.

Dr. Mark Yarbrough
President, Dallas Theological Seminary

The Scriptures are clear about our privilege as believers to prepare others as spiritual multipliers. Ken Horton's book, *Faithful and Focused*, puts the "meat on the bone" about how to accomplish that mission. As we explore the examples of Jesus and the apostle Paul, the "how to" becomes clearer to us. My experience in learning to wisely launch spiritual multipliers gave me an up-close experience with the truths explained in this book. This is not theory, but practical truth that works in the pressures of business leadership. This intentional preparation enabled me to begin a life-changing ministry among men who embraced the command of Christ to "go and make disciples of all nations."

During my last years in business leadership, I would often tell Ken my most fulfilling hours, apart from my family, were spent investing in multipliers. It is still true today, now that I enjoy the flexibility of retirement.

Kirk Blackmon
Retired CEO, Blackmon Mooring & BMS CAT

In an age of dumbed-down faith and easy-going beliefs, *Faithful and Focused* resets the bar of commitment where it needs to be. This ought to be required reading for every follower of Christ. My friend Ken Horton has done a magnificent job of blending practical biblical help as he explains the process of making a disciple and being a disciple. I'm going to buy six copies—one for myself and one for each of the men I am mentoring/discipling. This is one of the very best books I've read on discipleship.

Dennis Rainey
Founder of Family Life with his wife Barbara
Co-author of *Choosing a Life That Matters* and *The Art of Parenting* (with wife Barbara)

Ten years ago, I shared hours of discussion with Dr. Ken Horton about intentional, strategic discipleship while studying at Dallas Seminary. During weekly conversations, I gained biblical understanding, theological perspective, and relational insight, which continues to shape my life and ministry. When I returned to teach at STEP in Haiti, I began to incorporate these truths in the spiritual formation ministry with our students and with fellow pastors throughout our nation.

Now, it is refreshing to read Dr. Horton's book, *Faithful and Focused: Maximizing the Privilege of Discipleship.* This book is rooted in the reality of the joyful privilege of being part of God's purpose each day in ways that impact eternity. These chapters remind me of our conversations and friendship, providing wisdom and motivation for any believer who desires to embrace the model and mandate of Jesus: sharing the Gospel graciously, encouraging other believers toward maturity, and preparing faithful people as fruitful multipliers. It is a divine strategy for every nation and every generation.

Andrikson Descollines, Th.M.
Academic Dean, STEP Seminary, Haiti

If you want to read a book on discipleship that is written by one who has lived with these truths for many years and has given his life to the privilege of discipleship, you need to read this book by Ken Horton. It is scholarly, biblical, and practical, reflecting the joy of preparing multipliers.

Dr. Bill Thrasher
Professor, Moody Bible Institute

Dr. Ken Horton has provided us with one of the most engaging and comprehensive books on discipleship and multiplication I have ever read. Each chapter is packed with insightful gems and takeaways and could stand alone as worthy of an entire book. Don't miss his appendix on "Theological Insights for Multipliers," which reflects a wealth of fruitful conversations. While a lot has been written on this subject, you will gain a new understanding after digesting *Faithful and Focused*. I highly recommend it.

Susan Perlman
Chief Partnership Officer and Co-founder, Jews for Jesus
Board Member, MissioNexus

In our evangelical world, discipleship has been a much-abused word. Ken Horton's book, *Faithful and Focused*, is a serious and refreshing oasis on the subject—as though discipling involves disciplined personal engagement and great personal joy. As you read this book and embrace these truths, the blessing for which you were created will multiply.

Dr. Stu Weber
Pastor, Author of *Tender Warrior* and *Four Pillars of a Man's Heart*
Army Green Beret, Recipient of Three Bronze Stars

FAITHFUL AND FOCUSED

MAXIMIZING THE PRIVILEGE OF DISCIPLESHIP

KEN HORTON

FAITHFUL AND FOCUSED: *MAXIMIZING THE PRIVILEGE OF DISCIPLESHIP*

Copyright © 2024 by Kenneth F. Horton

All rights reserved, including the right of reproduction in whole or in part in any form, except for brief quotations in printed reviews, without prior permission of the publisher.

All Scripture taken from the NEW AMERICAN STANDARD BIBLE, Copyright © 1995 by The Lockman Foundation. All rights reserved. Used by permission. www.Lockman.org

Publisher Information
Kenneth F. Horton
P.O. Box 100486
Fort Worth, TX 76185

For more information or to contact the author, please email ken.ministrycatalysts@gmail.com or visit www.ministrycatalysts.com.

ISBN 979-8-9908096-0-4 (softcover)
ISBN 979-8-9908096-0-4 (eBook)

Cover design: Terry Dugan
Cover photo credits: Colorful Sky - Kavita @ Adobe Stock
                              Vineyard - Anna @ Adobe Stock
Editorial Team: Cristina Wright and Amy Sinnott
Interior design: Ben Wolf, Inc.

Publishing services provided by BelieversBookServices.com

First printing: 2024

Printed in the United States of America

ACKNOWLEDGMENTS

This book was forged through decades of relationships with family, friends, and faithful believers. It is dedicated to my wife, Kathy, a delightful wife, amazing mom and Gigi, and a fruitful multiplier who invested in our family, many women, and hundreds of children (especially 3rd graders). She is now with Jesus, and her impact still enriches our family, community, and decades of grateful friends. Many conversations with our children, Anna and Josh, strengthened the ideas and sharpened the communication throughout this book, echoing the wisdom they gained from their mom.

We were privileged to serve together for twenty-seven years in ministry at a church just twenty miles from my brother Ron, and his wife, Terri, who were pastoring a church and raising four children. As you will discover in this book, Ron and Terri had a pivotal influence on our lives and a life-changing perspective on discipleship. It has been a privilege to focus with them on preparing multipliers through Ministry Catalysts since 2011.

Pastors and ministry leaders in Texas, many parts of America, as well as in nations on several continents have embraced and equipped faithful people with the truths, priorities, and skills explored in this book. Discipleship discussions shaped by these concepts have been translated into languages spoken by over three billion people and are available for free download (*Launching Multipliers!* at www.ministrycatalysts.com). The feedback from key partners like George Hillman, James Womack, Grant Kahl, Jon Sherman, Tim Bach, Jim Smith, Tom and Lucia Howorth, Tom Lenning, Brian Givens, Dave Salsberry, and Bill Marshall has refined each chapter of this book.

Gracious insight from Dr. John Hannah, encouraging counsel from Cecil Price, editorial assistance from Mark Tobey, and wisdom from Dave Sheets and the team at Believers Book Services were pivotal blessings.

Each of the endorsers of this book has decades of life and ministry distinguished by intentional, strategic investment in spiritual leaders. Their example and encouragement continue to challenge me toward a strong finish. We share an abiding joy in the privilege of making disciples and look forward to celebrating this blessing forever.

CONTENTS

FOREWORD

I've always believed there are two main reasons believers don't make disciples. The number one struggle is we feel inadequate. This self-defeating message is whispered in our ears: *If others really knew how weak my quiet time is or the sins I am battling, they would never want me to mentor them.* Secondly, if we did start meeting individually to disciple a younger believer, what exactly would we do when we met? Discipleship is a mixture of affection and direction. We may know how to care for another person's soul, but what is the path of spiritual growth we are supposed to be leading them on? We all need some kind of specific content or curriculum to help guide the process.

In Ken Horton's excellent book *Faithful and Focused: Maximizing the Privilege of Discipleship,* he addresses these issues and so much more, educating and challenging us to a higher calling—that of being a "multiplier." This is what Jesus was referring to when he proclaimed in Matthew 9, "The harvest is plentiful, but the workers are few." Horton's mission is to answer Jesus's heart cry for more workers, giving us a profound treatise of what it looks like to multiply your life for Christ.

It's obvious to me that this volume is a product of Horton's decades of studying the Scriptures, learning from his mentors, and raising laborers through his discipling ministry. Let's unpack that: You'll take a unique and powerful journey through the "what, why, and how" of the Bible's mandate to all of us to "make disciples of all the nations." You'll have a front-row seat learning from the incredible interviews and biographies of past and present men and women who have taken the Great Commission seriously. And most of all, you'll gain practical insights from the "in the trenches" war stories from Horton's lifetime of reproducing himself in others.

Whether you're in full-time ministry, a student, a mom, a leader in your church or community—really anyone who embraces God's work in others (and yourself)—you will experience the "privilege of discipleship" Horton describes. And be assured, as you go through chapter by chapter on your own or in a small group, your theology will be deepened, your mind will be stimulated, your heart will be ignited, your character will be challenged, your vision will be expanded, and your "discipleship to-do list" will be filled with creative and empowering ideas.

Ready to become a multiplier for the person and purposes of Jesus Christ here on earth? If so, dig into this life-changing, ministry-changing, eternity-changing book. I exhort you to read thoroughly, reflect deeply, and renew your commitment to be "faithful and focused" in fulfilling the Great Commission.

Dr. Steve Shadrach
Founder, Student Mobilization
Global Ambassador, Center for Mission Mobilization
Author, *The Fuel and the Flame* and *The God Ask*

1

WHY ANOTHER BOOK ON DISCIPLESHIP?

At age eight, having heard a clear explanation of the Gospel, I trusted Christ for forgiveness and eternal life. Being raised in a nurturing Christian home and attending a church emphasizing spiritual growth, my life included Bible study, Scripture memorization, prayer, evangelism training, and frequent involvement in group activities. This was an environment appropriately associated with genuine spiritual growth encouraged by numerous books on discipleship.

Moments of gratitude for my salvation in Christ occurred in this positive environment, but the focus on performing external activities resulted in both discouragement and arrogance. Yearly youth retreats or an occasional catharsis known as "rededicating your life" provided opportunities to acknowledge my spiritual struggles and make a fresh commitment to be a "better" Christian. This renewed commitment focused on my efforts to do the prescribed activities, which contributed to my spiritual growth. While this repeated pattern may have impressed others, each new beginning left me struggling with anxiety, anger, and arrogance. My teen years pursued external spirituality with limited personal joy, reflecting an unwitting, fleshly desire to validate a relationship with God.

In 1968, my youth pastor contacted me about a classmate who had recently trusted Christ as his Savior. He asked if I would spend some time with Jerry to help him get started as a new believer. As a seventeen-year-old senior with a reputation as a spiritual leader—greater than the reality of my walk with God—I accepted the responsibility to help my classmate as a new believer. Excited about his relationship with Christ, Jerry diligently completed the weekly assignments that helped him study the Bible, and he took time to pray, deepening his understanding of his new identity in Christ. The results were remarkable! His gratitude for what God had done in his life deepened as the Holy Spirit worked. As he grew, my perspective on living as a follower of Christ began to change. In fact, we realized together how God's goodness toward us far outweighed our self-fueled efforts to gain His favor. These one-on-one conversations (discipleship) not only cemented our friendship but provided a foundation for fruitful years of ministry for both of us.

The opportunity to disciple Jerry personally gave me a fresh taste of life that was motivated by gratitude to God. Eventually, that experience was strengthened by training and practical experience with Campus Crusade for Christ during college. Opportunities during my years as an Air Force officer introduced me to people from other parts of the country who shared my interest in intentional spiritual growth. Throughout seminary and several years of youth ministry, one-on-one discipleship became a consistent priority. I assumed these partners would spontaneously begin investing in others. Yet, this rarely occurred, in part because our conversations focused on their personal growth without sufficient preparation for ministry with others. A second factor included an inadequate awareness of a chronic tendency to pursue spiritual activities in our own strength, reflecting our sinful nature. Paul shared his own struggle in this area in his letter to the believers in Rome:

> *"For I know that nothing good dwells in me, that is, in my flesh; for the willing is present in me, but the doing of the good is not."* (Romans 7:18)

Like Paul, perhaps Jesus's most fruitful equipper of disciples, we face the constant battle to accomplish spiritual results in our own strength. The problem remains that our understanding, our motives, and even our best ideas for effective discipling can be unreliable, even sinful at their core. It is not surprising that this fleshly perspective provokes comparison with others, fueling discouragement or arrogance. A posture of intentional dependence on God and an awareness of indicators of drifting toward the "default" of self-reliance is essential for enjoying the blessings of living by faith.

These dynamics prompted a decades-long examination and engagement with the concept of discipleship. Even though I had preached often on walking by faith, God sent me on a deep dive into the fruitfulness and joy of ministry that is only possible through intentional dependence on Him. I searched the Scriptures, sought Him earnestly in prayer, and tried to put into practice the principles He revealed through the process. This book reflects the insights God used to enlarge my understanding of the blessings that await those who join Him in His gracious work of spiritual multiplication. A vision for making disciples emerged: There is an authentic joy released in our lives as we equip spiritual multipliers with an intentional dependence on the Lord's gracious provision. Preparing multiplying disciples becomes a privilege infused with lasting joy!

Ultimately, the blessings of this journey led me to write this book to share this perspective on discipleship and the motivating joy with anyone eager to maximize their privilege in serving Christ. My goal is to shorten the learning curve toward a life of intentional dependence on God, proactively addressing the persistent vulnerability of our sinful flesh which undermines both our fruitfulness and blessing in all aspects of ministry. Cultivating dependence on God, whether described as living by faith, abiding in Christ, or keeping in step with the Spirit, is the rudder that guides the development of faithful believers who become fruitful multipliers.

There are biblical truths that must be obeyed, important skills that will enrich ministry, and theological understanding that will strengthen our hearts. But the benefits of every dimension of discipleship can only be embraced by faith and unleashed with joy as we engage in the ministry God has prepared for us. Discipleship is never a short-term project, but a life-changing privilege with earthly blessings and eternal rewards. After not seeing this clearly enough for years, this book reflects lessons learned the hard way, but now enjoyed in ways I hope will help you maximize this privilege of discipleship.

Complementary, Not Competitive Perspectives

A search of Amazon's books on discipleship reveals dozens, which are often available for next-day delivery. Jesus's command to "make disciples" has captured the attention of many followers of Christ. This emphasis stimulates celebration and reflects God's gracious tapestry woven throughout the history of the church. Also, it provides a context for vigorous debate about the definition of terms, dynamics of the process, and preferred strategies for the disciple-making modeled by Jesus and mandated for the twelve disciples shortly before His ascension.

The term translated *disciple* in the New Testament indicates various nuances in different contexts.[1] Intrigued learners sought an understanding of Jesus and His message. But others who struggled to grasp and accept the invitation Jesus offered abandoned Him when He clarified the reality of a relationship with Him (John 6:60). The "come and see" (John 1:39) phase lasted several months and led to "follow me" (Matthew 4:19), where learners became believers who were discovering how to grow in this relationship.[2] These followers, including dozens of men and women who supported Jesus's ministry personally and financially, shared Jesus's traveling ministry (Luke 6:12-17, 8:1-3). He taught them in group settings, often in large crowds. These followers would have been among the hundreds Jesus met with after the resurrection (1 Corinthians 15:6) and the 120 who gathered in Jerusalem in one place after Jesus's ascension (Acts 1:15-2:13).

After months of teaching and following a night of prayer, Jesus selected twelve from among the larger group to receive His focused attention (Luke 6:12-16). These devoted servants responded to Christ's invitation to "be with me" (Mark 3:13-14) and actively participated with Him in His ministry (Matthew 9:35-10:42; Luke 9:57-10:24) as preparation for their mission as faithful multipliers (Matthew 28:19–20). The night before Jesus's crucifixion, He challenged these men to "remain in me" (John 15:5-7) as they spread the message of the Gospel.[3] Jesus's ministry reflected both His faithfulness to all His followers and a strategic focus on a few He intentionally prepared for a life of leadership through spiritual multiplication. Luke's account of the early church (following the death and subsequent resurrection of Jesus) in Acts refers to believers as disciples more than twenty times without any qualification,[4] indicating every believing follower of Jesus is a disciple.[5] While apostolic leadership, represented especially by Peter, James, and John was significant, Paul eventually became the central figure in the spread of the Gospel throughout the Roman world. His letters provide the most extensive insight into the practical realities of how Jesus's command to make disciples can be obeyed.

Surprisingly, Paul, the master multiplier in the early church, never used the word *disciple* in his sermons or any of his many letters; however, he does exhort Timothy and Titus to follow his example as they share the Gospel, encourage believers toward maturity (Titus 3:1-11; 2 Timothy 4:1-5), and prepare faithful people who will continue this pattern of multiplication (Titus 2:1-8; 2 Timothy 2:1-7). The biblical model of discipleship *embraces faithfulness to all and a focus on a few.* Every genuine follower of Christ needs consistent encouragement toward maturity by spiritual leaders who are equipping faithful leaders for this dynamic strategy. *These pivotal aspects of discipleship are not competitive, but complementary. Faithful multipliers enlarge the capacity within a group to encourage growing believers toward maturity.* Before examining this biblical model closely, key concerns that impact-focused discipleship, require careful attention.

Real Concerns

Discussion of focused discipleship, especially in a one-on-one setting, often engages specific concerns: *apathy* among believers not receiving such intentional encouragement, *arrogance* for those who are blessed to experience this focused nurture, and *persistent pressures of life and ministry* impacting the availability of time and energy needed for such personal investments. Apathy and arrogance are issues for believers (whatever their specific growth experiences) and must be addressed wisely. In addition, the pressures of life and ministry can disrupt the focus needed for preparing multipliers.

The Drain of Apathy

Paul's letters to believers in several churches, and to young pastors he had personally discipled, dealt with many issues related to growing weary or apathetic about the mission. The remedy in almost every case for Paul was to keep the focus on Christ and all He has accomplished for those who trust Him. Letters to churches included repeated exhortations about spiritual growth (Ephesians 4:1-3, 25-32; Philippians 1:27-30, 2:12-16) as did those to key leaders (1 Timothy 4:6-16, 6:11-16; 2 Timothy 1:8-15, 2:1-7; Titus 2:1-8, 15, 3:8-11).

In one classic passage, Paul tied the remedy for potential apathy directly to keeping our focus on the death and resurrection of Christ:

"For the love of Christ controls us, having concluded this, that one died for all, therefore all died; and He died for all, so that they who live might no longer live for themselves, but for Him who died and rose again on their behalf." (2 Corinthians 5:14)

What a powerful word of encouragement for anyone facing the peril of apathy! The remedy to apathy is our spiritual focus, not our current ministry opportunities. This grateful, rational response to Christ's sacrificial death, knowing we will each give an account of our lives to Christ, addresses the persistent possibility of apathy.

The Hazard of Arrogance

Arrogance, a challenge for any believer, also requires consistent attention during the disciple-making process and throughout the Christian life. Arrogance is more than a distraction; it is dangerous because God promises to oppose those who are proud. For the believer, He deals with arrogance in painful, loving discipline. Proactive humility, which protects from the consequences of arrogance, is not rooted in the relational setting of the discipleship experience but will be encouraged by the authentic example and exhortation of a humble leader. Humility formed in us by the Holy Spirit and modeled and cultivated wisely in discipleship relationships protects growing believers from painful consequences and invites God's blessings. Paul repeats the urgency of demonstrating humility during progress toward maturity and preparation of multipliers (Ephesians 4:1-3; Philippians 2:1-11). Peter's struggles with humility added distinctive emphasis to his emphatic teaching about this pivotal element of leadership (Luke 22:24-27, 56-62; 1 Peter 1:13-2:12, 5:1-11).

The Distraction of Persistent Pressures

Pastoring an evangelical church in Fort Worth, Texas, amid the blessings of nurturing a young family, the challenge of pursuing a PhD program, and the opportunity to be the chaplain for the Texas Christian University football team multiplied the time pressures for me and my family. My response was to cease investing in men in one-on-one conversations so I could focus on preaching on Sundays, leading group studies for men, and working with the elders to lead and shepherd a growing congregation. These fruitful ministries helped believers grow spiritually and enjoy influence in their relational spheres. There was meaningful progress toward maturity for many without an intentional priority on launching strategic multipliers. My schedule was full, and God was blessing my efforts, but I was not preparing people to nurture their hearts and develop their skills for spiritual multiplication.

Pastors, business and professional leaders, teachers, homemakers, business leaders, and skilled workers all know the time challenges involved in significant pursuits. Paul exhorted his readers to make the most of their settings for maximum impact for Christ (Ephesians 5:15; Colossians 4:5). Wise choices with limited time resources are critical when responding to Jesus's command to make disciples. Loving your family, demonstrating credibility in your vocation, serving God with gratitude in your relationships, and embracing the renewal and rest people need are the contexts in which intentional discipleship must be pursued. This requires a disciplined devotion to seeking the Lord in prayer, asking for and following His wisdom with clarity about ultimate values.

An analogy helps unpack this issue. If you have a container with limited capacity alongside a few large rocks, many smaller stones, a pile of sand, and a large pitcher of water on a table, how do you maximize the empty container? The order of placement is determinative. Large rocks first, then stones, then sand, and finally water always yields the best outcome.

The same remains true in all of life. Your most valued endeavors are like large rocks; while meaningful issues, enriching lifelong term, are the stones. Sand and water are the aspects of life that provide daily joy but with less enduring significance. With constant time pressures in life, deciding if and when the large rock of preparing multipliers will be placed in your "container" becomes a critical decision. After decades of ministry, the joy of progress toward maturity was significant, but my container did not have room for the intentional preparation of multipliers. Almost twenty years ago, I chose a reset, making sure the big rock of intentional preparation of multipliers became the starting point for my weekly schedule. Even though it comprised only a few hours each week, focusing on personal investment in multipliers became a key priority. This priority did not displace the rocks of leading and blessing my family, encouraging others toward maturity, and building relationships with people who needed to trust Christ; however, unfruitful meetings, discussing insignificant differences, or watching sports had to be limited to free up a few hours each week to invest in one-on-one faithful multipliers. This choice enriched both my joy and enlarged the team of leaders prepared to encourage others toward maturity.

As the leader of a large pastoral team, I had many conversations with staff about how to manage their 168 hours a week. In each situation, individuals make choices, and choices always reveal values. If you think you do not have time for your family but never miss watching Sports Center, honesty becomes the first step toward wisdom. I began to make time for preparing multipliers when a fresh view of the value of intentional multiplication strengthened the motivation needed for this strategic process.[6]

A second pressure also relates to values. We live in a world that is constantly squeezing believers, and especially leaders, to pursue measurable and timely results. Attendance, budgets, building programs, and expansion of discipleship groups are common topics for discussion when church leaders gather. Comparison is hard to avoid. Pressure to perform impacts business, academics, athletics, and ministry. This reality makes a significant investment in a faithful person an expression of confidence in an ancient ministry model.

While Jesus taught large crowds, encouraged scores of fellow travelers, and had time for individual conversations during a three-year walking tour of Israel, He made training a dozen key leaders His consistent priority. Paul taught and preached in synagogues, marketplaces, and homes, but his many years of missionary journeys, helping believers toward maturity, became the context for persistent emphasis on preparing leaders to be fruitful multipliers. Both Jesus and Paul equipped a few multipliers as their central strategy for multigenerational, global impact. While there have been amazing spiritual awakenings that involve large numbers in the history of the church, the impact has often been impressive and beneficial, but with diminishing significance.[7] God has used mass movements at pivotal times, but intentional investment in faithful multipliers sustains Christ's model for building His church. An emphasis on results does not impugn the character of any leader, but it does recognize a pressure that is impacting ministry methodologies. Bigger and quicker are not the criteria of the Judge and Master of every disciple—Jesus Christ. Making certain we are following Christ's example and intentionally focusing on helping those we serve to grow spiritually, while carving out time to invest in multiplication, strengthens fruitfulness and joy amid the persistent pressures of life. This approach also sustains the needed motivation to stay on the hard path of equipping leaders for all aspects of ministry (2 Timothy 2:3-7).

Clarity About "The What" With Emphasis On "The How": Becoming A Part of God's Tapestry

After examining numerous books and resources on discipleship, I began to initiate conversations with people who shared my passion for this priority. They often mentioned the books and seminars that stimulated their interest, prompting a question about whether the book or seminar addressed the *why, what,* or *how* of discipleship. The *why* and *what* were prominent in their responses, but rarely focused on the *how*. Then I would ask if they had clarity about the values and skills that they needed to guide a person toward maturity in Christ, often resulting in an uncomfortable silence. This book seeks to explain the *what* of intentionally preparing multipliers with a persistent emphasis on the *how* of the process. *Faithful and Focused* unpacks biblical patterns, spiritual values, relational skills, theological perspectives, transforming priorities, and enduring motivations for a faithful believer who desires to maximize the joyful privilege of discipleship while growing more and more reliant on God's gracious provision and power (Matthew 6:24; Ephesians 5:16; Colossians 4:5; 1 Timothy 6:17-19).

When I first began to learn about intentional discipleship in college, I remember thinking, *why hasn't anybody done this before?* No one suggested it as a new idea, but I had never heard about it in such a clear, motivating way. My basic understanding of the Bible gave me a little perspective on the connection between what I was learning and how God had worked in the church to leverage the model of ministry pursued by Jesus and Paul. As a history major, I eventually took courses on medieval German history and the Reformation, providing a deeper appreciation of the ways God's grace prevailed amid religious confusion and human failure. He used faithful, courageous, and forgiven people day by day and century by century. Each chapter will conclude with *An Encouraging Thread* from this tapestry of grace, putting a spotlight on God's work of multiplication through the centuries. The biblical message is consistent, but the structures and methods have adapted for the new wine of salvation in Christ that is enjoyed by each generation of believers; however, the mission endures—make disciples!

2

EXAMINING BIBLICAL EXAMPLES AND EXHORTATIONS FOR EQUIPPING DISCIPLES

Enthusiasm about discipleship among many churches and parachurch organizations has increased substantially in recent years. This blessing encourages careful consideration of the examples and exhortations which guide obedience to Christ's command to make disciples of all nations (Matthew 28:18-20). Key transitions in the Old Testament, such as Moses to Joshua (Exodus 17:8-14; Numbers 13-14; Deuteronomy 31:23) and Elijah to Elisha (1 Kings 19:19-21; 2 Kings 2:1-15) illustrate the development of spiritual character, shared experiences, and personal encouragement in cultivating leaders. Building on these enduring values, the examples and exhortations of Jesus and Paul provide the defining pattern for preparing intentional spiritual multipliers, which is commanded and often discussed but less commonly pursued.

Jesus's Dynamic Ministry

The gospel accounts portray Jesus's ministry as a relational marathon, lasting more than three years. He engaged people individually (John

1:43-51, 3:1-21, 4:7-38), in small groups (John 4:39-43), and large crowds (John 6:1-14), sometimes teaching (Matthew 5:1-7:27), often healing (Mark 2:1-12, 3:1-6, 5:1-13), frequently explaining their need for forgiveness (John 3:1-4:42), challenging people to join Him in evangelism (Matthew 4:19), and gaining a reputation as a "friend of sinners" (Mark 2:15-17). He persistently demonstrated faithfulness to the multitudes, speaking and connecting with them while pointing to the blessings of knowing and serving God (Matthew 5:1-12). His ministry leveraged relationships between friends (Matthew 4:18-22; John 1:40-51) and soon gathered traveling companions.

As Jesus's public ministry gained momentum, He made a strategic transition. After a night of prayer, Jesus chose a dozen men (Luke 6:12-19) who became His designated apostles or "sent ones" also known as the Twelve (Matthew 10:1-2). Continuing a public ministry, engaging many in various settings, Jesus devoted more and more of His time to preparing this handful of faithful followers to embark on the history-changing mission of spreading His message and modeling His ministry throughout the world.

Robert Coleman delineated this preparation process with brevity, clarity, and penetrating perspective, identifying eight sequential elements: selection, association, consecration, impartation, demonstration, delegation, supervision, and reproduction.[1] Jesus selected a few, spent extended time with them, established the challenge of being apostles by addressing a hard-hearted priority of their own interests, gave them His love, encouragement, admonishment, and restoration, showing them what serving God and blessing people involved, and sent them out for ministry opportunities. He commissioned them to follow that same pattern in the Spirit's power after His return to heaven. Coleman emphasized Jesus's strategy as not being centered on "programs to reach multitudes, but focused on developing men who the multitudes would follow."[2] Paul makes it clear that faithful men and women, not just organizational leaders, enjoy the privilege of being part of this life-changing purpose (Titus 2:1-8).

Jesus's Climactic Mandate

Jesus modeled *faithfulness to encourage* people to begin a relationship with God and grow toward maturity with a strategic *focus on preparing multipliers* to expand both dimensions of discipleship. During the forty days before His ascension, the resurrected Jesus met with the apostles as a group three times (John 20:19-29, 21:1-13), talking personally with Peter after breakfast in Galilee (John 21:15-23). As Jesus's ascension approached, the remaining eleven apostles gathered on a mountain in Galilee to receive His final exhortation (Matthew 28:16-20). This brief challenge, known as the Great Commission, clarifies the scope of Jesus's authority in giving this command—as well as where, how, and how long this mandate should be obeyed.

Absolute Authority

Absolute statements are easily understood. All things exist through Jesus (John 1:3), all things are subject to His authority (Ephesians 1:19-22), His name is above every name (Philippians 2:9-11), and, thus, these foundational leaders and those who join in this mission have His enduring support. Jesus's authority is never a limiting factor in the fulfillment of this climactic command to make disciples. Every generation of believers responds to this challenging mandate as the only reasonable response to the One with ultimate, universal authority.

Global Scope

Jesus tells His disciples to "go to all nations." This participle functions as an imperative because of its association with the command "make disciples." Acts 1:8 affirms this mandate when Jesus exhorts His disciples to be His witnesses in Jerusalem, Judea, Samaria, and the world—the mission remains unchanged. People who are not faithful and focused on discipleship where they presently live will rarely begin this pattern because they go somewhere else. Starting in the present, wherever you live, encourage people to trust Christ and make progress toward joyful maturity while identifying and preparing faithful people as multipliers.

During the exile in Babylon, Jeremiah instructed the people of Israel to live productively, blessing those with whom they shared life (Jeremiah 29:5-10). Though not their preferred earthly home, Babylon became an opportunity to serve God amid challenging circumstances. Wherever we are, in seasons of joy, hardship, preparation, or fulfillment, our calling is to make disciples. A humble, hopeful response to painful experiences can enlarge a person's credibility as an intentional, strategic multiplier. The best indicator of a future engagement in God's purposes is our response to current opportunities.

Consistent Priorities

Two additional participles identify essential elements of obedience to Jesus's command. First, believers in Christ should be baptized as an affirmation and celebration of a new spiritual identity established when they trust Christ for salvation. Jesus's instruction addressed the reality of new life in Christ, not the ritual celebrating the reality. As new followers of Christ develop this relationship through prayer, learning from God's Word, worship gatherings, and interaction in group settings, they enjoy the privilege of clarifying their hope in

Christ (Colossians 4:5-6; 1 Peter 3:14-16). Proactive involvement in structured and spontaneous opportunities for personal evangelism defines a key aspect of preparing a multiplier. Obedience to Christ's discipleship mandate incorporates lifestyle evangelism as an enduring priority.

Second, Jesus exhorts the twelve disciples and all believers to teach others what they have learned during their time with Him. While Jesus taught many aspects of a life pleasing to God, His inter-action with the twelve affirmed truths and demonstrated skills for preparing multipliers essential for obedience to this command. *It is a process of learning to be Jesus's disciple*, not a mentor's disciple. Whether described as abiding in Christ, keeping in step with the Spirit, or imitating God, following Christ as His disciple becomes a path of faith. Distinguished by humility, gratitude, obedience, and joy as God's partner in daily life, the spotlight remains on Jesus and can only occur through supernatural empowerment.

A disciple's life must be rooted in intentional dependence upon God's provision and strength. The apostles and those who gathered in the Upper Room understood that they needed God's help through His promised Holy Spirit. This realization becomes critical because any spiritual endeavor has the possibility of inflaming fleshly desires to impress people or even God. We easily drift toward self-reliance that is so "normal" because it is our default position in life. This may explain Jesus telling His disciples they had hard hearts (Mark 6:52, 8:17). An authentic, though imperfect, example of dependence on God is the heart of any discipleship relationship preparing someone to launch other multipliers.

Enduring Urgency

Christ promised to be with His followers through the Holy Spirit until the end of the age.[3] His strategy and priorities will endure as believers have an opportunity to encounter people who need Him, encourage believers who need to be nurtured, and equip those willing to invest in multipliers. Any ministry will be enhanced by fruitful people no matter its size, scope, or strategy. Being prepared to share Christ's message and launch spiritual multipliers is a blessing believers can continue if they can interact on a phone call, go to a coffee shop, or use a computer for a conversation. Until Jesus returns, or we join Him in heaven, putting this priority on the front burner of life is a great privilege, yielding earthly and eternal blessings.

Paul's Fruitful Ministry

Saul was a young Pharisee with fierce hostility toward the church in Jerusalem (Acts 23:6). He watched as Stephen respectfully engaged the Sanhedrin (Acts 7:2a), carefully describing the history of Israel's rejection of their prophets (Acts 7b-50), and, boldly confronting them with their lawless, brutal murder of Jesus (Acts 7:51-53). Filled with rage, the council and the crowd drove Stephen out of the city, stoning him as he beheld the exalted Christ and followed His example by praying for his executioners. We are introduced to Saul as he holds the robes of the mob while heartily approving Stephen's brutal death (Acts 7:58, 8:1a). Saul became the key persecutor of the Jerusalem church, viciously imprisoning followers of Jesus (Acts 8:1b-3).

As the church expanded in Samaria and the city of Damascus, an enraged Saul received permission from the High Priest to travel to Damascus to arrest believers so they could be brought to Jerusalem for punishment (Acts 9:1-2). On the journey to Damascus, the risen Christ confronted this persecutor with a blinding light and a piercing question, "Why are you persecuting me?" When Jesus identified Himself and gave Saul instructions for the completion of his journey (Acts 9:3-18), Saul took his first steps of faith as history's most passionate Christian evangelist, church-planter, and intentional, multiplying disciple.

After Saul's initial growth under the guidance of Ananias, he became a powerful witness for Christ in Damascus (Acts 9:23). During that season, Saul received revelation from the risen Christ in Arabia before returning to Jerusalem three years later (Galatians 1:15-18). Saul's unique discipleship experience gave him a foundation for a lifetime of exceptional fruitfulness. Just as He chose the twelve and nurtured them in obedience, Jesus selected Saul, spent time with him, encouraged his devotion to God's purpose, and continued to work through the indwelling Spirit to prepare His newest apostle.

Saul, who later came to be known as Paul, was *faithful* regardless of his ministry opportunity.[4] He remained committed to his calling even when serving God in the shadows for years in Tarsus between a turbulent visit to Jerusalem (Acts 9:26-30) and his ministry partnership with Barnabas in Antioch (Acts 11:19-26). He was *available* to be a helper for Barnabas in Antioch, *intentional* as he strengthened believers in Antioch and others through extensive missionary journeys, *teachable* as he learned from Ananias, Jesus, and Barnabas while his *heart* for God's mission was sustained in the face of immense suffering and eventual martyrdom as Christ's apostle to the Gentiles.

Paul modeled humility by being a partner under Barnabas's leadership (Acts 13:2,7) before Luke, the writer of Acts, changed the delineation to Paul and his companions (Acts 13:13) and then Paul and Barnabas (Acts 13:42-43). Distinguished by joyful gratitude to God (2 Corinthians 2:14-16, 9:15, Philippians 1:3-8, 3:1, 4:4) and relentless in urging intentional dependence on God (Romans 6:11, 12:1-2; Ephesians 1:19, 5:18; Philippians 2:12-13), Paul impacted major cities throughout the Roman Empire. During several long and arduous journeys throughout the Mediterranean, Silas, Timothy, Epaphroditus, Titus, and others traveled with Paul, helping him nurture local churches while learning from him the truths and skills essential for spiritual multiplication.

Paul's Final Exhortations

More than three decades after Jesus commanded the twelve to make disciples of all nations, the apostle Paul wrote a second letter to Timothy from a prison in Rome. Unlike Paul's earlier house arrest, the Roman "death row" chamber convinced Paul of his approaching death.

In such situations, only the most critical issues matter. Paul focused on exhorting Timothy to pay attention to humility, courage, and faithfulness as the foundational stones of spiritual credibility. He later clarified the importance of enduring the hardship of a hostile spiritual environment by valuing healthy relationships strengthened by biblical truth. At the conclusion of the letter, Paul acknowledged that he had met his life goal of running the race of faith and finishing strong. Paul exhorted Timothy to cultivate a clear perspective as he pursued his ministry and declared his commitment to finish his race with courage, confidence, and joy (2 Timothy 4:7). In this stirring challenge, Paul reminded Timothy of the pattern he had seen and learned in their collaboration in ministry.

Clarity on the Value of Multipliers

Paul began this final letter to Timothy with fatherly encouragement for his protégé who was still working through the challenges of pastoral leadership in a hostile environment. Exhorting Timothy to employ the spiritual blessings provided with confidence in Jesus's faithfulness, Paul showed sensitivity to Timothy's tears, timidity, and shame (2 Timothy 1:4,7,8). Though not a bold leader, Timothy became a fruitful pastor, affirming that people with all kinds of personalities can be God's instruments (1 Thessalonians 3:1-8). The exhortations Paul gave this young leader emphasized Jesus's power, not Timothy's vulnerabilities.

Persistent Dependence on Jesus's Strength

The person and ministry of Jesus shaped a strategy for equipping his multiplying disciples that was sustainable only by a full reliance on His power amid spiritual conflicts and pressures. Four commands clarify Paul's strategic instruction (2 Timothy 2:1-7). First, Timothy must *experience God's power* through the same power that raised Jesus from the dead (Ephesians 1:19). Relying on the power of God is essential for effectiveness in the strategy of making disciples. It is a supernatural process from start to finish. If this command is neglected, the pursuit will be an exercise of the flesh that may impress people but result in little to no impact on someone's life. Ultimately, God will not be pleased with that approach, and the person or people involved will miss out on the joyful blessings of supernatural transformation.

An Intentional Process with a Strategic Purpose

With that essential principle established, Timothy received Paul's second command to *entrust to faithful people the spiritual truths* he had learned. After watching Timothy engage in ministry over several years, Paul had great confidence that his younger apprentice knew what to teach in this strategic ministry. The spiritual treasures Paul had faithfully deposited into Timothy ensured his investments would continue to benefit the next generation of multipliers.

Paul knew Timothy was clear-minded on the most important truths necessary for developing a maturing, multiplying follower of Christ. In both spiritual and practical endeavors, people rarely pursue something they do not understand. Most people learn best when they discuss and practice the content and skills required with a more experienced guide with firsthand experience. That had been Paul's strategy in discipling Timothy. As Timothy depended on God's strength and continued to learn in each group or personal interaction, he was better prepared to take the baton of multiplication from Paul and pass those lessons on to others.

A Sobering Challenge with Joyful Blessings

The third command is to *endure hardship* (2 Timothy 2:3-7). The form of this imperative implies it is a shared hardship with Paul and with others who obey the previous commands. The response of faith in Jesus embraces the *dedication* required of a soldier who unflinchingly follows the orders of his commander. As a soldier for God, our commander is Jesus Christ. Though all commands of Jesus apply to His followers, it seems appropriate to connect this exhortation from Paul with Jesus's climactic mandate to "make disciples." Soldiers obey orders without hesitation because they have a preemptive commitment to the commander and his mission. Throughout human history, soldiers have given their lives for the temporal protection and prosperity of their families, tribes, or nations. Paul leveraged that reality in the use of this metaphor, calling followers of Christ to boundless dedication to follow clear commands from Christ Himself. The promised reward for such unswerving devotion carries eternal value.

But the path of hardship requires more than dedication. Paul described the *discipline* of an athlete as critical for fulfilling the mission—not merely a monumental moment of personal sacrifice, but a steady exercise of focus and intentionality essential for athletic excellence. While discipline involves a range of factors, the one nonnegotiable for a person who pleases God is exercising daily faith (Hebrews 11:6). Faith means we know and obey God without regard to our feelings, circumstances, or cultural pressures. It is the only path that is pleasing to God and the necessary "rule" for a person engaged in multigenerational multiplication. We must believe God is both powerful enough to use us and wise enough to give us a counterintuitive plan in which a *focused investment in the faithful is a critical step toward being faithful to the multitudes.* It takes faith to follow the strategy used by Jesus and Paul.

Paul further illustrates the blessing of discipline by using the metaphor of a farmer. Even a limited observation of what it takes to cultivate and maintain successful farms, dairies, or ranches validates the *diligence* required for enduring progress. The hard-working farmer enjoys the "first fruits" of such efforts. That same principle is true of making disciples. Developing and nurturing people, as in running a farm, requires hard, intense labor, often influenced by circumstances outside our control, but with the promise of genuine joy in an eventual blessing.

The relational investment involved in equipping people for faithful ministry is hard work, too, but yields a harvest of right-eousness and joy when approached through the discipline of faith (John 4:35). While elsewhere Paul describes the eternal rewards of faithful ministry (Philippians 4:1; 1 Thessalonians 2:19–20; 1 Timothy 6:17–19), the joy of intentional preparation of spiritual multipliers enriches our earthly lives and fuels faithfulness in all aspects of ministry. What a wise and gracious God to include this dynamic in His plan for spiritual influence!

Confidence That Jesus Still Chooses Multipliers

Paul concluded his exhortation with a fourth command to ponder these truths and let Jesus guide the response (2 Timothy 2:7). *Jesus still chooses multipliers.* Our opportunity is to present this privilege clearly with our lives and words and let Jesus draw others to obey Him. When a multiplier invests in a faithful believer, both people are Jesus's disciples as they continue to prepare for greater fruitfulness and joy in serving Him. Pressuring someone to work through a process of spiritual growth without the assurance that they are responding to Jesus's leadership distorts the reality of spiritual multiplication. Jesus is the only person worthy of genuine disciples.

Commitment to Help All Believers Grow Toward Maturity

As he finished his letter, Paul challenged Timothy to be faithful in ministry, encouraging believers toward maturity. In 2 Timothy 4:1-5, Paul exhorted Timothy with nine commands to guide his ministry in Ephesus: preach the Word, be ready in season and out of season, reprove, rebuke, exhort, be clearheaded, endure hardships, be faithful in evangelism, and fulfill your ministry. These commands reflect the ministry Paul had among the churches he planted throughout the cities of the Roman Empire. Paul preached the gospel, taught in synagogues, city centers, and lecture halls, wrote letters of spiritual nurture, and traveled throughout the Mediterranean region to encourage and strengthen believers. Desiring to demonstrate his faithful commitment to individuals, small groups, and large crowds even in the face of intense persecution, Paul painted a compelling picture of helping people grow in spiritual maturity. Timothy would have grasped the complementary blessings of both dimensions of discipleship, *faithful to many, and focused on multipliers,* without any confusion about the blessing of both.

An Encouraging Thread

Henrietta Mears (1890-1963) became a dynamic Christian leader who invested in a wide range of ministries that helped children, students, and adults make progress toward maturity and encouraged key leaders to embrace the challenge of preparing multipliers. After several years of teaching science and math in high school and helping establish a flourishing children's ministry at a Baptist church in

Minneapolis, Mears moved to California in 1927 to pursue children's ministry at the First Presbyterian Church of Hollywood. Until she died in 1963, Mears nurtured local church ministries with global impact. The children's group grew from 450 to over 2,000 through her exceptional leadership. When she could not find a curriculum for her ministry, she started writing her own and sharing it with others, a venture that came to be known as Gospel Light Publishers, a publishing organization that impacts children's ministry among evangelicals throughout America.[5] In 1953, she wrote *What the Bible Is All About,*[6] which became a best-selling resource. In that excellent work, she captured her biblical insights in the memorable style that fueled her exceptional ministry. In 1961, Mears launched Gospel Literature International (GLINT) to provide resources for global ministries.[7]

While much of her time was given to young women, all who were involved in her large ministry learned from a godly example and dynamic insights. Her scope of teaching spread to teenagers and young adults, and her strategic motivational skills influenced hundreds of outstanding leaders who became pastors and ministry leaders. She became a mentor and motivator for young leaders who had a profound impact on the global church in the twentieth century.[8]

Bill and Vonette Bright lived with Miss Mears for eleven years.[9] The earliest gatherings of students eventually became known as Campus Crusade for Christ, which started in her home. The Brights introduced Billy Graham to Mears. Graham struggled with his confidence in the trustworthiness of God's Word early in his ministry. His pivotal commitment to God's Word occurred at Forest Home Christian Conference Center also founded by Mears.[10] She also encouraged him to pursue the pivotal first Los Angeles crusade in 1949. Graham said Mears "had a remarkable influence on my life" and was "one of the greatest Christians I have ever known."[11] Jim Rayburn, the founder of Young Life, modeled his ministry to high schoolers on what he saw in her ministry. Mears served as a bridge builder among leaders, an expert at graceful engagement, collaborating with leaders like Dawson Trotman (The Navigators), Bob Pierce, (World Vision), and Cam Townsend (Wycliffe Bible Translators) during the early years of these transformative ministries.[12]

God greatly used Henrietta Mears, a gifted teacher and developer of multipliers. She was an organizational genius with a rare capacity to identify and motivate strategic leaders. This thread could extend for several pages listing pastors, parachurch leaders, and missionaries (as well as politicians and movie stars) who looked to Mears as a pivotal spiritual influence.[13] She helped launch scores of national and global leaders who encouraged multitudes and equipped multipliers, a bright thread in God's tapestry of fruitful multiplication.

3

FOUNDATIONAL VALUES FOR FRUITFUL MULTIPLIERS

Foundational values shape all aspects of the intentional preparation of spiritual multipliers. These values reflect both biblical instruction and practical experience. As in all spiritual endeavors, character remains essential, discernment critical, and priorities always necessary. When a person embraces *the importance of personal example, the impact of obedience to Scripture, the blessings of theological health, and the influence of genuine joy,* they are positioned to prepare leaders with multi-generational impact.

The Importance of Personal Example

The *example of a lead partner* functions as a thermostat in shaping the impact of conversations designed to prepare multipliers. This dimension of intentional discipleship is consistent with any mentoring relationship. As a mentor, spiritual or otherwise, your words, actions, and attitudes will be central elements of personal influence. Most parents discover their children will not always do what they say but almost always do what they do, especially if the doing and saying are in harmony.

Only a few specific statements by many excellent teachers during childhood, college, and seminary remain cemented in my memory. The way they pursued their teaching responsibilities and how they treated me and other students had lasting significance. Over the years, coaches, military commanders, pastors, and business leaders have modeled the path of wisdom and wilderness of folly in ways that encouraged and protected me in life's various environments.

Moses understood the significance of relational influence (Deuteronomy 6:1–9). Ezra modeled this pattern when he studied and practiced the law of the Lord before teaching the people (Ezra 7:10). Paul's exhortation to imitate him emphasizes "things you have learned and received and heard and seen in me" (1 Corinthians 11:1; Philippians 4:9). The command to "make disciples" requires authentic transmission of what Jesus taught His disciples by words and example, *emphasizing that the believers we equip are Jesus's disciples, not ours.* Paul anchors his ministry with the Thessalonian church in the power of the Gospel and the impact of his example in their relationship leading to an impact far beyond their city (1 Thessalonians 1:4-9, 2:7-12), illustrating a pivotal principle: a *godly example stimulates expanding influence.*

There are many ways to encourage a person in a discipleship context. Some are simple. Being prepared for the conversations is significant. Even being on time for the meetings will communicate you value the person's time and the privilege of entrusting spiritual truth to a faithful partner; however, consistently practicing the truths discussed in each session is the foundation for an environment of continuing growth for each person. The flexibility to address pressing challenges becomes an opportunity to lead by example. Helping a person face a problem at home or a difficulty at work, even if the conversations in the discipleship process must be paused, validates a commitment to prepare a person for long-term fruitfulness, not just complete a discipleship process. Godly character is validated when a lead partner discusses a personal struggle and God's help in his or her own life. Such transparency demonstrates humility and encourages spiritual growth.

The humility that is essential for fruitful ministry empowered by God is not optional. Leaders humble themselves as a doorway to God's blessings (Luke 22:25-27) or they will be humbled by God's discipline (1 Peter 5:6-7). The example of authentic humility anchors all other insights and encouragements, promoting maturity and preparing multipliers. Humility reflects a consistent embrace of two biblical truths simultaneously: Jesus's exhortation to "Abide in me... apart from me you can do nothing" (John 15:5) and Paul's reminder of "I can do all things through Him who strengthens me" (Philippians 4:13). Maintaining this dual focus will ensure that the believer enjoys the blessing of being exalted by God. Humility is rooted in consistent thoughts about Jesus rather than an ever-changing perspective of yourself. If humility is not taught by example, both maturity and multiplication will be compromised.

The importance of our example is revealed in how we pursue the best interests of a discipleship partner; however, one of the most significant elements of genuine humility is revealed in celebrating the times when you learn from the insights and examples of the preparing multiplier. Having worked through these conversations with scores of faithful people, God has used each person to expose biblical insights or specific steps of wisdom. Consistently affirming this mutual blessing with partners strengthens their confidence that God can use them in significant ways. Humility is not optional, but inevitable. People will either humble themselves so God can lift them up, or their pride will result in God opposing and humbling them with painful consequences (Proverbs 3:34; Philippians 2:9–11; James 4:6–10; 1 Peter 5:5–7).[1] Humility is expressed in how we respond to God's Word, treat people, endure hardship, and enjoy relational blessings. While content is important in the multiplication process, the cultivation of humble dependence on God will shape our relationships with others as the core of the transformation God desires.

A few years ago, I enjoyed discussing our process with a gifted pastor in a large city in Asia. Our many conversations addressed significant issues in the context of his family and ministry, resulting in encouraging growth in both areas. As we continued to explore the importance of humility, he mentioned an issue he faced with another leader on his team. When we drilled down on the specifics, it seemed likely the ministry associate struggled with pride. I asked my friend, "Is there a person in his life that God can use to help him see the importance of humility?" After a long silence, I continued, "Is he seeing humility in your life clearly enough to guide him toward God's path of blessing?" After another pause, my friend began to think more honestly about his own life. As he intentionally humbled himself before God, changes in his life allowed God to influence his ministry associate and his family. This emphasis on character, especially humility, is pivotal for preparing a faithful person, not just finishing a program.

The Impact of Biblical Obedience

Fruitful multipliers *engage with the specific biblical passages* when preparing others for this privilege. Paul described Scripture as God's provision for clear direction, convicting rebuke, constructive correction, and affirming instruction for believers (2 Timothy 3:16–17). Paul outlined this dynamic pattern regarding God's purpose for believers to be thoroughly equipped for the good work prepared for them. This process is rooted in revelation from God Himself, literally "God-breathed." This does not mean God dictated the words for the original authors, but the Holy Spirit worked through dozens of authors as they wrote what God intended, while using the language, cultural context, education, and spiritual intimacy shaping their lives. The impact of any Scripture reflects both the truth of the passage and the spiritual condition of the person hearing the truth.

A passage teaching at one point may rebuke at another, and what provides correction for one person may offer training in righteousness for another. Scripture does not change, but the application of its truth distinctively touches people who are changing throughout life. The psalmist David describes *spiritual and emotional renewal* for those who obediently embrace the perfect, right, and pure truths of God's Word (Psalm 19:7-11). Whether restoring the soul, making the simple wise, rejoicing the heart, enlightening the eyes, or clarifying perspective on our choices, biblical truth offers an enduring blessing for God's servants. Three thousand years later, the need for healed souls, practical wisdom, joyful hearts, and a clear vision of what God values has never been more urgent.

In his New Testament epistle, James declares hearing God's Word without doing what it says to be spiritually disorienting (1:22–25). When people disregard this truth, they reach a point where deciding to do what God says becomes a hollow substitute for actually doing what He says. That misstep results in chronic self-deception, compromising the ability to perceive one's true spiritual condition.

When a discipleship conversation engages God's Word and moves from observation to interpretation to obedient action, God's wisdom guides toward the choices that are pleasing to Him and result in transformation (James 1:5-7). God eagerly gives us the wisdom we need to navigate the many vexing situations in life. The source of true wisdom is primarily in the Bible, but God also guides us through the indwelling Holy Spirit and the counsel of godly people. If humility before God provides the foundation for preparing multipliers, the integrity revealed in consistent obedience to God's Word becomes the *path* that leads believers toward fruitful maturity, pleasing God, and blessing people.

The value placed on obedience to Scripture connects to the significance of memorizing Scripture. Learning from Jesus as one of His disciples includes following His example. Jesus perfectly modeled Moses' instruction to Joshua to meditate on God's Word as the path of spiritual success (Joshua 1:8). Jesus Himself dealt with temptation by quoting truth and confronting Satan's distortions (Matthew 4:1-11; Deuteronomy 6:13, 6:16, 8:3; Psalm 119:9-11). He corrected the confusion of the Sadducees about the resurrection (Matthew 22:23-33; Exodus 3:6) and answered the Pharisees' question about the greatest commandment (Matthew 22:34-40; Leviticus 19:15; Deuteronomy 6:5) with specific passages. Jesus used biblical truth to explain why he cultivated relationships with people who were considered spiritual outcasts (Matthew 9:12; Hosea 6:6). Jesus voiced his anguish on the cross by quoting from a psalm of lament (Matthew 27:46; Psalm 22:1).

As we follow Jesus with biblical truth hidden in our hearts, meditating on Scripture strengthens our ability to obey God on the path of blessing, stimulates worship (Colossians 3:16), and focuses prayer (John 15:7). In our finances and especially for our family, we embrace it in our hearts and minds. Memorizing verses for each conversation and reviewing them throughout the process seeks to establish a lifetime pattern.[2]

Whether reading, studying, or memorizing Scripture, a believer should remember the Holy Spirit superintended the revelation of Scripture (2 Peter 1:20-21) through forty authors in three languages during 1,500 years. He indwells believers to teach, guide, and encourage them (John 14:26-27, 15:26). As we pray, He prays for us with divine wisdom (Romans 8:26-27). Gratitude for this "inside job" becomes a wise starting point for every exposure to God's Word.

The Blessings of Spiritual Health

God uses the influence of a humble partner and the impact of God's truth in obedient people to strengthen the *fruit* of theological discernment. For decades I have observed believers dodge theological discussions to avoid conflicts with others. Unhealthy arguments about theological issues are certainly possible, as they are in other aspects of life. The remedy to this unfruitful dynamic is not avoidance, but wise engagement as Paul and Peter taught through their letters (Colossians 4:2–6; 1 Peter 3:14–16). The reality that others may disagree with us, even to the point of hostility, informs the interaction and promotes progress during discipleship conversations. The benefits of clarity and confidence about the biblical support of one's theological perspectives help believers face even difficult conversations with Christ-like gentleness and respect.

Paul also emphasizes the importance of sound doctrine or teaching rooted in God's Word, which results in healthy lives and relationships (1 Timothy 1:3-7.) Paul challenges Timothy and Titus to hold fast and be devoted to and nourished by spiritually beneficial truth. This requires both proactive affirmation of truth and persistent rejection of any teaching inconsistent with God's Word (Titus 1:9; Jude 3–4). It demands theological clarity (2 Timothy 1:13), which encourages both the confidence to affirm the truth and to remain calm when engaging those who may disagree with respect, grace, and wisdom. When people are unsure of their beliefs, they pound the table, often out of frustration. But those who are settled in their convictions are free to understand the perceptions of others, so their questions can offer an opportunity to evaluate differing views while discussing them with a gracious, well-prepared person.

Moral clarity is another fruit of healthy doctrine (1 Timothy 1:10, 6:3). In a world swamped by confusion, rooted in rebellion against God's character and even creation itself (including the question, "What does God's Word say about this issue?"), can provide a consistent, though provocative perspective. While ever-changing cultures have opposed biblical moral values in diverse ways throughout human history, the hostility has fluctuated wildly; however, blessings for human society flow from integrity, compassion, humility, and sacrificial love rooted in biblical truth. Loving God and loving others are countercultural, but powerfully significant in a world where Christ's mission joins the authenticity of its messengers with the credibility of the message. Christ's ambassadors are most useful when their lives provoke honest questions in their listeners and followers. That is true even when those questions are couched in hostile terms. Moral consistency and clarity anchored in healthy theology and expressed through compassionate people are essential dimensions of God's gracious purpose. Healthy doctrine and a life pleasing to God are intrinsically linked (Philippians 1:9-11; Colossians 1:9-10; 1 Peter 1:13-16).

A final benefit of good theology is the motivation it provides for fruitful ministry. Sound doctrine clarifies a believer's calling to be a faithful servant of God. That privilege, embraced by faith with a grateful heart, ensures lasting accountability for those destined to be joint heirs with His glorious Son, Jesus Christ. For creatures made in God's image and entrusted with both abilities and opportunities to join in His purpose, good doctrine emphasizes each person will give an account of his or her life. Both Jesus and Paul taught how we live in this life will matter in eternity (Matthew 6:19–21; Luke 12:34; 1 Corinthians 3:10–4:7; Timothy 6:17–19). This often-neglected doctrine motivates a believer to invest in others and begin each day with joyful anticipation for what God has prepared during work, family time, recreation, and other activities. These benefits reflect the theological "connective tissue" incorporated in each fruitful discipleship conversation. A discipling partner can then examine important issues and gain clarity about different views of theology. There are orthodox essentials that define evangelical theology such as God's eternal, Trinitarian existence, the full deity and perfect humanity of Jesus Christ, the total sufficiency of Christ's death on the Cross, the sinfulness of human beings, and the authority of Scripture. Other theological issues clustered around these truths are areas in which Christians may disagree. Both the essential and debated matters can be discussed in ways stimulating clarity and confidence regarding biblical truths. This process enhances the capacity to have respectful, honest conversations with people who see things differently.

The primary means of holding fast to sound, healthy doctrine involves a careful, obedient study of Scripture. When this fruitful dynamic joins with intentional conversations, encourages good questions and respectful discussion, and maintains humility before God, believers follow Paul's example of multiplication. They also amplify the blessings of sound doctrine.

The Influence of Genuine Joy

As believers enjoy the blessings of obedient integrity rooted in humility before God, they begin to stimulate questions from family and friends. The night before His crucifixion Jesus taught His disciples to abide in Him and how, by doing so, they would bear fruit and be filled with joy (John 15:5–11). Paul repeatedly exhorted the Philippian believers to embrace joy in the Lord (Philippians 2:18, 3:1, 4:4). In a world squeezed by anxiety and anger, joyful people have a magnetic and intriguing attractiveness. This is amplified when they respond wisely and respectfully to hostility and criticism (1 Peter 1:6-9). When people ask me about the primary emphasis of our ministry-to-ministry leaders and growing Christians, I usually answer, "We seek to help believers enjoy being God's co-laborer so many people will be curious enough to ask their questions about either receiving Christ or serving Him."

Fruitful multipliers are thankful for the privilege of investing in others. When Paul described Timothy, Titus, and Epaphroditus, he talked of their character, commitment, and eager willingness to partner in Christ's mission (Philippians 2:19-30; 1 Timothy 4:12; Titus 2:7–8). Peter reminded spiritual leaders that they serve because they want to, not because they must (1 Peter 5:3). Preparing people for ministry enriches this life and prompts worship for eternity. This blessing produces joy, which cannot be contrived or hidden. In a world gripped by anxiety and roiled by hostility, a person filled with joy and prepared for gracious conversations becomes an instrument God uses to attract people to His Son Jesus!

Values Shape Methods

These spiritual values can be pursued in different learning environments. Many evangelical churches emphasize large group teaching, small group discussion, and community ministry activities, as well as personal spiritual growth experiences like prayer and Bible study. All of these can contribute *to progress toward maturity* and should be encouraged as part of meaningful discipleship.

When the discussion turns to *preparing fruitful multipliers*, the debate centers on whether this biblical priority is best pursued in group settings or one-on-one conversations. Both approaches can embrace the values delineated in this chapter. The issue hinges on which environment becomes most fruitful in preparing faithful leaders to equip other multipliers. The primary options are small groups, triads (groups of three), or one-on-one relationships

There are outstanding models of small group discipleship that add an element of multiplication through the preparation of leaders for new groups. For instance, Jim Putman and his associates have developed excellent resources[3] framed by a life-cycle model of the Christian experience. The small group approach presents a path for incremental progress toward maturity in a nurturing relational environment and involves multiplication through the preparation of key leaders to take other groups of believers through the twelve-week, five-lessons-per-week training manual.

Chris Swain and Robbie Gallaty also offer a group discussion experience called Replicate, with thirty-two chapters of beneficial content aimed at both progress toward maturity and preparation of multipliers equipped to model and lead discussion of the book with a new group.[4] Like Putman's strategy, their plan affirms the relational and spiritual benefits of group environments designed for churches, which value the making of discipleship. While acknowledging there may be a place for one-on-one discipleship in leadership development, Swain and Gallaty express a concern about a possible ping-pong dynamic in one-on-one settings where the conversation devolves into a counseling session. These authors perceive greater productivity, faster growth, lesser intimidation, increased group accountability, and following Jesus's example of group discipleship as benefits of their group discussions.[5]

Church-based programs require persistent support by church leadership in both time and corporate focus. As with any group strategy, participants will miss meetings and the continuity of the discussions frequently will be diminished. If ten people are in a group, a few will talk too much, a few will want to talk more, and some will happily avoid engaging completely. While there are spiritual benefits for participants, the challenge of cultivating fruitful leaders usually involves intentionality and consistency not possible in group settings.[6]

Greg Ogden proposes a triad model for spiritual multiplication, involving three people with a "keeper of the covenant" who is guiding the process relationally while working with two believers at a time.[7] He notes (as key advantages) wisdom in numbers, more natural participation for the disciples, and a shift from a hierarchical dynamic to a relational dynamic. He provides some excellent insights on discipleship, making this a valuable resource; however, the advantages of triads must be weighed against several realities. Most importantly, any potential for a hierarchical dynamic does not depend on the size of the group but on the genuine humility of the lead partner. As noted earlier, a *lack of humility by a leader will sabotage spiritual progress in any environment.*

In practical terms, managing adjustments in the schedules of three people (sick children, last-minute work requirements, etc.) can make the process complicated and uneven as individuals have unavoidable, last-minute conflicts. Momentum in meaningful conversations can be difficult when only two people are adjusting their schedules. Adding a third person increases this reality significantly.

With two people in a conversation, the skill of expressing one's views is consistently strengthened. In a group of three or more, especially when one person tends to dominate, the opportunities to voice personal thoughts clearly and confidently diminish. If people cannot explain their views or don't feel free to raise honest questions in a conversation, they likely do not understand them well enough to implement them consistently or explain them to others.

When coaches evaluate potential quarterbacks for college or professional teams, they usually have the player stand at a whiteboard and draw plays while explaining them before going to the practice field. There is no place to hide at the board or in the game. One-on-one discussions give a lead partner a similar opportunity to explore spiritual truths, enlarging the capacity of both partners to discuss such issues in future environments, especially where there is disagreement. This is a critical skill for lifestyle evangelism and the preparation of multipliers. Some in a group may be hesitant to ask all of their questions, especially if an individual is substantially less knowledgeable about Scripture than the other participants. That tendency will be compounded if one person dominates the discussion. Not only is the less engaged person hindered in spiritual growth, but all participants may be less likely to develop skills in asking questions. Learning to be more like Jesus includes strengthening listening skills and wisely asking questions to help a person think about and discuss the important issues in life. Freedom to discuss personal issues (problems at home or work) may be hindered by the presence of a third person. Although great trust can exist among three or more friends, it requires all participants to have a generous measure of transparency and a strong commitment to confidentiality. *The conversations of a group usually reflect the lowest level of individual trust.* Ogden's emphasis on the importance of trust, the centrality of biblical truth, and the value of accountability are important in many ministry settings; however, one-on-one conversations provide a distinctively beneficial environment for people to ask their questions, honestly unpack their consistent struggles, and learn how to discuss their thoughts on critical issues.[8]

Engaging in a one-on-one conversation requires a less sophisticated relational and leadership skill set than other environments. Balancing the conversation between three people (or more in a group approach) as well as listening carefully and being sensitive to the body language of multiple people is not an easy task. The number of people capable of a vigorous, fruitful conversation with one person is much larger than those who can be highly effective with more than one. After decades of ministry experience and because of these practical realities, I have determined to maximize my remaining years by prioritizing one-on-one discipleship that is focused on intentional, strategic multiplication.[9]

There was also a personal dimension to that choice. As a lead pastor, I perceived the decision to abandon one-on-one discipleship primarily as a time issue. But another factor I did not see clearly at that time was that only a few of the men I had spent time with had gained sufficient confidence to equip others for intentional multiplication. We had worked through important truths, but the emphasis on their spiritual growth did not communicate the values and skills needed to prepare others for such ministry. While discouraging, it revealed I had not personally experienced these values and skills with the intentionality required to affirm and model them myself.

For over a decade, that nagging realization remained unaddressed. Throughout those years, my brother Ron, and his wife, Terri, served in a fruitful pastorate in a church in our county. Unlike me, he made intentional discipleship a priority during those years as a pastor and learned much about the process of preparing a person for this privilege. His enthusiasm during our discussions about discipleship eventually led to my agreement that small groups can help people grow spiritually, but preparing spiritual multipliers is pursued most effectively in a one-on-one context that is shaped by a firm commitment to continue this priority with other faithful people. During my last few years as a pastor, a priority on launching multipliers as they prepared to equip others for the same privilege enriched all aspects of pastoral ministry.

My preference for one-on-one discipleship does not diminish the joy that churches and individuals have found through group models. My reservations about group models are practical more than biblical. Jesus pursued both a distinctive group environment (reflecting rabbinical patterns in His culture) and an individual focus in many situations. When fruitful believers are enjoying the privilege of launching multipliers with different approaches, it should be celebrated. Each disciple of Jesus should make the most of their opportunity.

An Encouraging Thread

John Wesley (1703-1791)[10] became a pivotal spiritual influencer in the latter part of the eighteenth century. His father served as an Anglican rector and his mother, Susanna, became a powerful spiritual influence on her fifteen children. Though nurtured in this religious environment and stimulated by spiritual discussions with fellow students at Oxford, he remained unsettled in his relationship with God.[11] He traveled to the British colonies in America in hopes that a missionary endeavor might give him the spiritual clarity and confidence he desired. His observation of the unshaken faith of Moravian families during a terrifying storm on the voyage had a great impact.[12] Wesley continued to interact with Moravians during his difficult time in Georgia and when he returned to England. Their example was the context of Wesley's transformational experience in 1738 at Aldersgate in London. Listening to the reading of Luther's commentary on Romans, Wesley trusted Christ alone to forgive his sins.[13]

The example and the joy of an intimate relationship with God in his mother and the Moravians became pivotal elements of God's work in Wesley. In the following years, Wesley and Whitfield vigorously debated their different views on God's work of salvation. Whitfield emphasized larger evangelistic gatherings and Wesley developed an extensive network of small group gatherings, cultivating spiritual growth and accountability in the wake of extensive evangelistic preaching. They both valued teaching Scripture, though their theological differences regarding God's role in drawing people to salvation persisted. It is telling that Wesley spoke with affection and appreciation for his friend at the funeral services for Whitfield in London.

Whitfield's approach became a catalyst for revival meetings that were centered on biblical preaching. His approach, exemplified by Billy Graham and others in the twentieth century, eventually spawned the development of helpful discipleship resources for people who responded to the Gospel in crusades and other similar meetings.

Wesley's group discipleship approach reflected his investment of 250,000 miles of travel, mostly by horseback.[14] Each group followed a rigorous method, emphasizing accountability in practices of personal piety and resulting in the derisive name Methodist, eventually embraced by the denomination launched after Wesley's death. The current emphasis on group meetings for discipleship is building on Wesley's strategy, which followed a model he observed among the Moravians.[15]

Wesley remained engaged in the spiritual challenges that faced England to the end. On February 24, 1791, six days before his death, Wesley wrote a letter to William Wilberforce, an evangelical Christian and chief advocate for abolishing slavery in the British Parliament. Wesley had written *Thoughts Upon Slavery* in 1774, and in his last days, he challenged Wilberforce to follow the example of Athanasius in opposing the "execrable villainy" of slavery, reminding the young politician, "If God be for you, who can be against you?" Sixteen years later, Wilberforce became a key factor in abolishing the slave trade throughout the British Empire.[16] From preaching in the fields to developing hundreds of small groups to influencing Parliament, the thread continues—all for God's glory!

4

ESSENTIAL SKILLS FOR
FRUITFUL MULTIPLIERS

When our children entered their teen years, an older friend with grandchildren gave me and my wife, Kathy, some profound perspective. He assured us our children had been listening to our words for years. They knew what their parents thought, but the years before they departed for college offered an opportunity to discover *their* thoughts.

He urged us to major in the art of asking good questions rather than repeating our exhortations. Although we had valued questions in relationships and ministry settings for years, the urgency of helping our children prepare for life, marriage, parenting, work, and ministry energized our desire to sharpen both listening and questioning skills. Soon, our goal each day prioritized asking questions that were rooted in what our children communicated, verbally and nonverbally, with the hope that we could eventually smile and say, "I like the way you are thinking." What we learned in that process not only enriched our family but affected every aspect of our lives and ministry.

Many people and resources stimulated learning in this critical area. James Smith, a friend since our years at seminary, wrote a dissertation on Jesus's intentional use of questions. He ultimately developed a seminar and other resources as well as a book on coaching, which explores the pivotal impact of questions in helping people understand and pursue their passions and responsibilities.[1] As I learned about asking helpful questions in my family and ministry, I became a ministry coach in an intensive four-day program at Dallas Seminary that was designed for leaders and their spouses. The entire experience, driven by questions, helped the participants see the past, present, and future and reflect on each phase with greater honesty and renewed hope.

Several years later there was an opportunity to teach (with my brother Ron) a course on "Developing Leaders through Mentoring and Coaching" at Dallas Seminary. Eventually, the course became part of a doctoral program (DMin.) at Singapore Bible College. At each step, a closer examination of the impact of careful listening and wise questions yielded greater benefits. Books on coaching almost always contain a chapter on listening and asking questions, and online resources also reinforce the insights explored in this chapter.[2]

As a person pursues intentional discipleship, especially in a one-on-one conversation, two relational skills enrich each discussion: *careful listening* and *helpful questions.* Careful listening often becomes the source for wise questions, which stimulate fruitful interaction. These skills are also essential for believers who embrace lifestyle evangelism. When we give people an opportunity to share their reasons for rejecting the Gospel or disagreeing about a theological issue, that freedom (centered in grace) increases the possibility for more authentic, and at times, searching conversations. That's the point at which the possibility for genuine spiritual growth emerges. Freedom to ask honest, personal questions becomes critical in a discipleship relationship.

Careful Listening

Attentive listening communicates value for a person and enlarges opportunities for mutual encouragement and spiritual growth. Three levels of listening contribute to helpful conversations: *informal, intentional,* and *intuitive.* Each requires an engagement that is rooted in a genuine interest in discovering what a person thinks and values. These levels have a cumulative benefit, with informal listening, and energizing intentional listening, which strengthens intuitive listening.

Every conversation offers opportunities for *informal listening.* Whether at work, during recreation activities, walking in your neighborhood, or taking part in church activities, perceptive listening yields insights for casual conversation as well as future opportunities for spiritual significance. Discovering what people in your sphere of influence value will open opportunities. Genuine interest in a person creates space for people to share a blessing, unload a burden, or wrestle with struggle, sometimes initiating a deeper conversation. Cultivating informal listening skills in your home enriches life's most significant relationships and enlarges spiritual influence. The discernment to avoid disruption in the casual banter of life may require you to take a mental note to inquire about a comment privately.

Another benefit of informal listening is the discovery of opportunities for encouragement. When you observe someone act or speak wisely, affirming the person can have an enduring impact. Good listeners enjoy hearing and watching people for encouragement more than correction.

Intentional listening is a biblical value that expresses respect with a dynamic impact on people (Proverbs 10:19; James 1:19, 3:1, 12). This hard work requires discipline and attention not only to what is said but also to nonverbal expressions. Communication involves more than just words. In fact, words make up only 7 percent of communication; 38 percent is tone and voice, and 55 percent is body language.[3] How people perceive our attentiveness impacts their willingness to remain open or continue in conversation. That's why patience becomes necessary as a listener gains insight about the other person, not just "getting to the point." A skilled listener will develop instincts that are sensitive to these nonverbal elements. The best listeners often make notes after a conversation in preparation for the next meaningful interaction. That level of intentional listening will strengthen relationships and provide wisdom and reassurance for the listener (Proverbs 17:27–28).

Intuitive listening begins by seeking perspective from what is not said or directly expressed. When personal circumstances are described, repeated experiences may suggest patterns, offering better understanding. Sometimes a possible cause-and-effect dynamic suggests a pattern impacting future progress. Emotional flashes (anger, optimism, enthusiasm, or discouragement) become markers for heightened or future discussion. As you listen in this way, your gentle questions may encourage people to face what they already sense and are expressing in ways more instinctive than rational. In other words, a listener must value silence and resist the urge to move the person beyond their uncomfortable moments prematurely. As one sharpens these listening skills, a person may begin to see "red flags" or have "hunches" about what is happening in a person's life. Resisting the tendency to assume a definitive conclusion and allowing these intuitions to guide respectful questions helps pace the discussion and not rush the experience.

It is not surprising that people struggle with effective listening. In a world of distractions and noise fueled by an overdose of technology, hearing is difficult, and actual listening is rare. Often, real meaning is obscured, so any additional questions or answers are less helpful. Silencing the phone, finding a quiet corner, and praying for God's help are positive preludes for any personal conversation. Spiritual issues like anger and folly also sabotage the ability to listen and may create further damage in difficult conversations (Proverbs 14:12, 12:15, 18:2). Anger is a human reality. It is the response to hurt in a world where everyone experiences wounds—real and perceived. Contentious situations offer distinctive spiritual opportunities for life change. Promptly and wisely addressing internal anger will increase the capacity to listen, especially with difficult people.

There are also personal hindrances. Even when listeners overcome the distractions noted above, they may begin to prepare an answer while processing what is being said. Anticipating a response may ambush the conversation. Are we listening to respond, or listening to understand? The mental discipline required for intentional and intuitive listening is incompatible with multitasking. People need to be reassured that we are listening carefully and with empathy. Children are especially gifted in detecting compromised attention. *When we are listening, people know it. When we are distracted, they see it before we do.*

While careful listening positively benefits any relationship, it is essential for those who equip multipliers. Listening and asking questions, reflecting the thoughts of your partner, enriches the relationship and stimulates growth for both people. These same skills sharpened through discipleship conversations are essential for gracious believers who have conversations with unbelievers. Good listeners invite questions and encourage honest conversations about life's most urgent issue: experiencing and enjoying a relationship with God by faith in Christ's payment for sin.

My wife, Kathy, served as a fruitful servant of Christ for decades. We shared the blessings of marriage and parenting as well as the fruitful privilege of preparing multipliers. She became my most influential teacher in the critical importance of listening. Family, friends, and casual acquaintances delighted in their time with Kathy. In the years since she joined her Savior in heaven, hundreds of people have expressed their love and gratitude for her life. Although I have heard many encouraging comments, the most frequent is, "When I talked with Kathy, she listened like I was the only person in the world." Reflecting on our years together, I benefited from her unique listening skills, making me keenly aware of how I need God's help daily to grow in these skills. Since He is the perfect listener (Psalm 5:1–3; John 11:41–42), my best days as a listener are ahead of me.

Helpful Questions

Excellent questions will often be the fruit of careful listening. Studying books on asking good questions can be beneficial, but knowing when and how to ask a question is shaped by wise listening and often becomes more fruitful than the best answer. When you give a good answer, your partner hears only a portion of what you say and will remember only a fraction of the response; however, a good question presents an opportunity for invigorating engagement as the person prepares verbal responses. The ideas proceeding from your partner's mouth may capture the concepts your answer would have addressed.

Affirmation of your partner's discerning insights becomes a powerful way to strengthen their growth. At other times, what seemed reasonable and clear in his or her mind may begin to unravel when expressed in words. A gentle, respectful question may provide a "redo" that encourages your partner's clarity and confidence in future discussions. To put this priority in other terms, *a person usually learns more when thinking and talking about a good question than when listening to a good answer.*

Traits of Helpful Questions

Helpful questions shape fruitful discipleship conversations. Several traits strengthen the value of any question. An *open question* cannot be answered by "yes or no" and often stimulates additional helpful questions within a conversation. Closed questions like, "Could you sell your car to pay off your debt?" may suggest a possible solution while limiting discussion of the wisdom and skills that are beneficial for future choices. Learning to frame open questions requires a willingness to slow down and embrace a bit of silence to leverage a significant interaction.

A *focused* question often becomes most beneficial. Answers may be complex, but targeting a question on a single issue will help the person respond without having to remember other follow-up tangents. Additional questions may be part of a fruitful conversation, but emphasizing one at a time yields greater clarity for both people.

Questions that invite *personal responses* are most likely to address issues from the perspective of the person involved. Opportunities to understand your friend's views will help guide honest conversations. Questions like, "How did you reach your conclusion?" or "What are possible ways you could deal with your concern?" (asked with respect and gentleness) can defuse a sense of interrogation and move a person toward a wise next step.

Finally, questions that are *illustrated by an engaging word picture* or common experience can guide a person to new insights, especially when they are connected to something mentioned by the person.[4] This encourages the person to perceive the issue with a fresh perspective, clarifying the real-world issue being addressed. Metaphors and other word pictures are also powerful for teaching, especially when framed by stimulating questions.[5] One example that is frequently used in preparing multipliers contrasts learning to fly an airplane with gaining the skills to teach others to fly a plane. Our methodology is designed to equip "flight instructors" who are capable of not only navigating a fruitful life in Christ but are equipped to prepare others for that privilege.

Purposes of Helpful Questions

Common purposes for questions that are fruitful in leading, mentoring, parenting, or launching multipliers are *probing, revealing, and clarifying*.

Probing questions stimulate the formation of encouraging relationships. When a probing question connects with genuine interest, people often begin to communicate more openly. Such questions are most effective when linked to something a person has expressed. Jesus uses a probing question when He asks His disciples "Who do people say I am?" and then "Who do you say I am?" (Luke 9:18, 20). If a friend mentions that credit card debt has become a problem, a probing question might be, "Can you describe how you normally make financial decisions?" When questions are focused and simple, a person often begins to communicate thoughts more clearly. The discipline to avoid suggesting a solution within the question is critical. Probing questions communicate a desire to know and understand a person and may expose a perspective that invites other questions.

Revealing questions, often stimulated by probing questions, help move beyond a difficult issue to explore possible solutions. Revealing questions are aimed at gaining a rational response and are best expressed without emotionally charged language. Jesus employed a revealing question when He mentioned seeing the "speck" in a brother's eye and neglecting the "log" in one's own eye (Luke 6:41). A revealing question for the friend who is struggling with a relationship conflict might be, "What are possible ways you may have contributed to this conflict?" Such questions are maximized when they prompt a discussion, anticipating future choices related to the issue. As options are explored, revealing questions may require time for reflection or even multiple conversations.

Clarifying questions are central to discovering biblical convictions that lead to wise decisions. When questions guide someone toward a specific action—addressing an issue—the situation remains an individual responsibility. One such question is, "What do you think you should do about this situation?" For the third grader who forgot his homework, the sixteen-year-old ticketed for speeding, or the friend struggling with a relational conflict, helping the person assume responsibility for a wise step toward a healthy solution ultimately enriches life. When ownership of actions appropriate in a situation becomes specific and clear, responsibility is encouraged. When joined with dependence on God for the implementation of the decision, the benefits are both practical and spiritual.

Hypothetical situations can also be instrumental in helping a person discover clarity. When you frame a clarifying question as a "what if" (as a likely or even an unlikely possibility), it may stimulate fresh perspective or creativity. Questions like, "What counsel would you give to a friend in a similar situation?" or "If you had responsibility for a business decision, what would be your first step in that process?" can be helpful.

In discipleship discussions, the lead partner can cultivate simple patterns to help a believer grow toward consistent responsibility. Expecting the protégé to be prepared (especially with Scripture memorization) and to initiate any schedule changes promptly are part of discipleship. Accountability regarding specific steps of obedience to biblical truths becomes a significant aspect of this process. In all situations, the person facing an issue must pursue needed changes with God's help.

If someone cannot explain their views in a conversation, it is likely they do not understand them well enough to practice the truth consistently. Medical residents are trained as they "make rounds" with experienced physicians who use questions regarding specific patients as a key element in their training. One-on-one discipleship discussions allow partners to explore spiritual truths similarly, encouraging a step toward obedience and preparation for spiritual opportunities in challenging environments.

Asking questions enriches conversations with people who are not yet followers of Christ. While preparation to affirm our hope in Christ should be essential, the wisdom and respect encouraged by Paul (Colossians 4:5-6) and Peter (1 Peter 3:14-16) suggest helpful answers about our hope in Christ and are often shaped by good questions. In fact, both passages assume the answers are in response to the questions (or hostile reactions) of people who do not have faith in Christ. The authenticity of a believer's life is foundational for a life that encourages questions with answers that point toward Jesus. Listening well and asking additional questions builds on this foundation.

An Encouraging Thread

Justin Martyr, born in Roman Palestine and educated in Greek philosophy, became a key apologist for Christianity in the second century. Justin recounted a conversation with an elderly man who exposed the weakness of his philosophic views and presented the gospel of Christ through the Jewish Scriptures. Justin observed the courage of Christians facing persecution and the kindness of believers toward others.[6] This respectful conversation became the model for Justin's influential evangelistic ministry. His writings reflect his deep faith in Jesus as a perfect fulfillment of the aspirations of Greek philosophy.[7]

Justin described a conversation with a Jewish man by the seashore near Ephesus as a pivotal example of the skills needed for both evangelism and discipleship. Known as *The Dialogue with Trypho,* Justin depicted an honest, respectful dialogue when profound disagreement existed.[8] The skills of listening, asking questions, and communicating clear answers are on display in this account of lifestyle evangelism.

Justin vigorously defended Christians against charges of being immoral atheists in a letter to the emperor. A second letter protested the injustice of executing Christians because of their faith. It is no surprise that he became a martyr for Christ in Rome in about 165. His unshakeable courage and faithfulness to Jesus's example (John 4:1-30), and the exhortations of Paul and Peter, encourage believers to present Jesus with gentleness and respect while preparing multipliers in a hostile world. An important thread for this generation.

5

A PARADIGM FOR HONEST, RESPECTFUL CONVERSATIONS

The ability to talk clearly about an issue suggests a defining indicator of a person's capacity for gentler and more respectful conversations, especially when disagreement occurs.

Fruitful spiritual interaction frequently flourishes when insightful questions are combined with calm, gracious answers anchored in an authentic walk with Christ. Decades of life and ministry confirm the adage "you can win arguments or win people, but rarely both at the same time." That pithy adage does not mean we neglect contending for our faith in Christ, but it does affirm the approach and attitudes modeled by Jesus and Paul.[1] Jesus engaged interested followers and hostile adversaries without being personally combative. In rare situations, Jesus used the language of rebuke to confront the distortions and hypocrisy of the religious elite (Matthew 22:22-33, 23:1-15). He did cleanse the temple and confront the Pharisees and Sadducees regarding His identity as God's Son and Israel's Messiah; however, those strong actions were not an impulsive reaction to a personal offense, but an affirmation of both God's holiness and redemptive purpose.

As a person grapples with the truths of Scripture, grows as an intentional and intuitive listener, and cultivates a capacity to ask wise questions, the opportunities for honest conversations about spiritual issues will become more fruitful. When our questions and attitudes communicate genuine interest in the ideas of other people, it increases the possibility that they will be comfortable making statements about their views and asking questions about our perspectives. While true in our most intimate relationships, close friendships, and casual acquaintances, conversations about common relational interests with strangers can also open doors for spiritual interaction. Most unbelievers sense and appreciate interest in their lives and personal situations.

Years ago, my wife and I enjoyed a tour of Chile, Argentina, and Brazil with several other couples. We experienced a delightful time sightseeing and stimulating conversations with friends. On a flight from Santiago to the Patagonian region, I sat next to a man who spoke English. My inquiry about where he grew up led to a discussion of the beauty of British Columbia. After a few minutes, I asked about his perception of the spiritual climate in Canada. He mentioned his unhappiness with a childhood experience in a ritualistic religious environment. I then asked what brought him to Chile. He enthusiastically discussed his significant career as an engineer for a mining company with operations throughout South America. My genuine interest encouraged him to help me, a nonengineer, understand a bit about his life. When I asked about his family, he described a wife he met in Chile and two children he loved. To a question about what he found most challenging in a multicultural marriage, his response addressed his wife's faith in Christ and her consistent attendance at an evangelical church with their children, usually without him. I asked if he had any interest in knowing what his kids heard at church. After a brief silence, he smiled and said, "Yes."

I outlined the gospel message with a simple diagram and several key Bible verses. He stated the message we discussed helped him understand all his wife had shared with him, but he was not ready to trust Jesus personally. I wrote my email and phone number on the napkin and asked him to put it in a place he would remember if our conversation came to his mind in the future. I explained the Bible reveals that God delights in drawing people to His Son, so he should not be surprised if his thoughts returned to our discussion. As the plane landed, I thanked him for educating me on the challenges of gold mining and assured him of my prayers for him and his family. After a warm handshake, we departed. Though I have not yet heard from him, my prayer is that he will eventually trust Christ, in part, because of a comfortable conversation facilitated by gentle questions, careful listening, and a clear explanation of the most important message in human history.

The conversation I enjoyed while flying 35,000 feet above Chile was shaped by a paradigm that encourages honest discussions amid real disagreement about spiritual matters. It diminishes the likelihood of an angry argument and often builds a fruitful conversation. It has four parts: (1) *personal affirmation;* (2) *asking questions* with the purpose of understanding the life and views of the other person; (3) *giving a helpful answer* respectfully and persuasively; and, (4) *asking another question,* allowing the person to continue thinking about their views while pondering your comments.

Personal Affirmation

When we *affirm* a person's willingness to discuss an important issue, we are acting in harmony with theological, biblical, and relational values that are honoring to God. Every person we meet is created in God's image and is a unique expression of His purpose (Psalm 139:1-6). Whether we fully understand others' experiences or perspectives, agree with their opinions, or enjoy their personalities, each person before us is so precious that Jesus left heaven and came to earth to pay for the sin separating them from their Creator (Romans 5:1-5; Ephesians 2:1-8). This divine initiative releases a faithful witness from personal competition or being offended by a negative response from a listener, ensuring the long-term best interests of the person remain the focus.

A gracious posture helps a believer consistently obey Jesus's exhortation to love people, even our enemies. Humbly pursuing relational peace with others (Matthew 5:43-48) increases our credibility, especially in conversations where we express honest differences. But that mindset does not mean the conversation will stay calm and peaceful. Gracious, respectful words may still provoke angry, harsh responses. Yet we must keep in mind that, as we treat others lovingly (as God commanded) and explain the gospel message with honesty and grace, their reaction will not ultimately be toward us. Always remember that our response may be part of God's work in drawing a person to His Son, Jesus.

During my years as a space surveillance officer with the Air Force, I had the blessing of significant conversations with many people. As my relationship with Christ became known, some people asked questions about the Bible, often leading to fruitful conversations. Others made mocking comments, never a surprise, but still difficult. My commitment to deflect harsh comments without personal offense became common knowledge among the people with whom I served. As I worked with those critics, and sometimes engaged in sports and other activities with them, opportunities to encourage and be helpful grew more common. Slowly, the dynamics of many of those relationships changed. At times, the most hostile people ceased being opposed to my views. Eventually, a few even asked me to pray for personal or family concerns, which led to spiritual conversations. *Initial opposition can often be an early indicator of openness to spiritual conversations, especially when their hostility does not sabotage our geniune, personal concern.*

Such an approach does not reflect a conversational method or merely good intentions. It is anchored in prayerful confidence in God's faithfulness and the power of His Word. Imprisoned in Rome, awaiting trial and guarded by a rotating cadre of elite Roman soldiers, the apostle Paul wrote to the believers at Colossae and urged them to pray that God would open doors for a clear explanation of the Gospel with anyone he encountered while under arrest (Colossians 4:2-6). Cultivating the environment of genuine respect that is pivotal to be fruitful, spiritual conversations requires God's wisdom and power, both of which are promised to followers of Christ. Praying for such blessings is critical for any spiritually significant conversation.

A gracious attitude toward others, especially when they are hostile, must be joined with a humble embrace of the reality you can learn from other people's experiences, education, and even objections. When we show interest in the skills and experiences of others, they sense our attitude and often become more open to ideas they would reject immediately during an argument. *Although people may not understand our explanations at first, they almost always grasp our attitude toward them as valued individuals.*

Engaging Questions

Careful listening is essential for discovering questions to help people evaluate and explain their views. As we understand the thoughts of another person, good questions can stimulate clear communication. My travels in Asia have given me opportunities for conversations with people from Hindu, Muslim, and Buddhist backgrounds. Though I have a cursory understanding of these religious and philosophical systems, my starting point involves asking them to help me understand the basic elements of their views. After listening carefully and asking honest questions, I gain insights about the religious systems that shape the lives of billions of people. But that's only the beginning.

Anyone desiring to begin these types of potentially life-changing conversations can master this approach as well. For instance, one question I have found helpful in opening the conversation is, "What is one thing you believe about a relationship with God or life after death that you would want a Christian to understand?" Demonstrating to them a genuine curiosity about their answers builds trust, which is key to more honest engagement. Often, an opportunity to ask a pivotal question rooted in their words shifts the discussion toward the distinctive truths of Christianity. Their willingness to listen to our thoughts can be directly connected with our attitude toward them and how we carefully listen to their thoughts.

As noted earlier, an analysis of Jesus's questions is instructive as we develop these skills. James Smith's dissertation evaluates more than 300 questions (allowing for some repetition in multiple Gospels) used by Jesus in His earthly ministry.[2] He identified six basic purposes for the types of questions (probing, revealing, and clarifying) that are described in the previous chapter, with some being a hybrid of two of the categories. The following introduces these purposes for questions with biblical context and current examples for each.

Questions to assist the articulation of thoughts, insights, and goals (Luke 9:20; John 1:38).

- "How can I be helpful to you?"
- "What would a fruitful ministry with young adults look like a year from now?"
- "How would you write the next chapter of your life?"

Questions to clarify issues, connections, or cause and effect (Luke 10:36; John 16:19).

- "What do you mean by 'balancing work and family'?"
- "If your conflicts with your supervisor remain unresolved, how will it impact your effectiveness and influence at your company?"

Questions to challenge the evidence of behavior that is inconsistent with stated values (Matthe 5:46–47; Luke 6:41–42).

- "Would I see the spiritual priorities you express if I examined your calendar/bank account?"
- "What would your wife/kids say is most important to you?"

Questions to reveal distractions or obstacles hindering growth (Matthew 6:25–28; John 4:35).

- "What seems to be blocking you from reaching your goals?"
- "Is there an experience that is creating doubt or fear about the situation you are facing?"

Questions to elevate perspective on personal significance or life opportunities (Luke 18:40–42; John 21:15–17).

- "What else could you do to strengthen a healthy relationship with your direct report?"
- "If money was not an issue, how would you invest your life?"

Questions to connect actions with consequences (Matthew 21:28–32; Luke 5:22–26).

- "How is your present behavior affecting your marriage?"
- "How will this decision impact your long-term influence with others?"

Good questions give insight about how to give answers, addressing specific issues. *The more a person talks about their thoughts, the more likely there will be questions and answers contributing to clear understanding and wise choices.*

Honest, Gracious Answers

When genuine affirmation connects with respectful questions, the conversation leans toward a third critical element of fruitful spiritual conversations: presenting clear answers, reflecting careful preparation, and communicating in gracious, persuasive language. Peter experienced the painful aftermath of denying his relationship with Jesus on the night of the crucifixion (Mark 14:66-72). Within weeks, Peter became a faithful witness to Christ's resurrection. Yet, the wisdom he gained from this embarrassing failure became part of the message that Peter wrote to strengthen the courage of persecuted believers (1 Peter 3:14-16). Knowing what these believers were facing daily, Peter exhorted his readers to be prepared to answer anyone who asks about our hope in Christ with gentleness and respect. Paul urged the Colossian believers to embrace opportunities to explain the Gospel clearly, boldly, and graciously (Colossians 4:2–6). Peter's teaching identifies three essential elements for clear answers to questions about the gospel message.

First, clear and persuasive answers require *careful study*. Reading books on apologetics[3] and exploring other resources to explain and illustrate helpful responses to common objections to the message of Christianity[4] are of great value; however, diligent study of God's Word (2 Timothy 2:15) is a core aspect of preparation for fruitful conversations.[5]

Second, Scripture emphasizes that simply *knowing* the truth of Scripture does not equip a person to teach it to others. In the Old Testament period, Ezra was responsible for reinstituting Israel's pattern of living that was established by Mosaic Law, following the Babylonian exile. He carefully studied the law of the Lord, practiced it, and taught the statutes and ordinances to the people (Ezra 7:10). Obeying the truth he learned expanded his capacity to explain the significance of specific instructions. Understanding and following God's truth is a fundamental dimension of pleasing God (Hebrews 11:6). Such faith releases the *practical wisdom* that God delights to give to those who humbly seek it (James 1:5–7). That dynamic response to God's Word distinguishes religious information from transformational truth.

This paradigm of study, practice, and teaching strengthens pastors, teachers, and others who explain scriptural truths in group settings; however, any parent, community group leader, or faithful believer who is encouraging a friend needs the wisdom gained from careful study and obedience to God's Word. Fruitful discipleship conversations flow out of the practical, specific obedience to biblical passages as both partners express their views, explore possible differences, and take steps of obedience.

A third essential for beneficial answers is found in Paul's exhortation to "let your speech always be with grace, seasoned with salt, so you will know how you should respond to each person" (Colossians 4:6). *This winsome grace contributes to "salty" persuasiveness.* Preparing to give answers with gentleness and respect by God's grace (1 Peter 3:14-16) amplifies the impact of any answer. Learning to share your thoughts on biblical issues in a relationship of trust and encouragement becomes a significant step toward communicating wise answers in any dynamic conversation. Such answers are forged through obedience to God's Word, as well as the humility and wisdom gained from learning from our failures.

Another Helpful Question

If you provide an answer with gentleness and respect followed by *another appropriate question*, you help people think about their views while considering new thoughts. One-on-one conversations offer a role-playing dynamic regarding ways a debated issue or specific concern can be addressed biblically. Thinking about a coherent response offers a rich learning experience. Whether probing essential or debated matters, honest questions and possible differences become opportunities to strengthen listening and communication skills. The "theological connective tissue" within each conversation strengthens faithfulness to Scripture, as well as wisdom for conversations with people who understand such issues differently.

In some conversations, there is a final element worth considering. Jesus made statements provoking questions from others. To the paralytic he proclaimed, "Your sins are forgiven" (Mark 2:5). To Nicodemus, Jesus declared, "Unless one is born again, he cannot see the kingdom of God" (John 3:3). Talking to the woman at Sychar, He asked a question disrupting the social norms, "Will you give me a drink" (John 4:7)? To the Pharisees, He proclaimed, "You will seek me and will not find me, and where I am, you cannot come" (John 7:34). Such statements seek to encourage responses or further questions, not stimulate animosity. There are situations where a believer can follow Jesus's example with a calm, provocative statement to amplify spiritual opportunity. At times, people may react negatively. If Jesus is the source of the animosity, it must not be taken personally (John 15:18).

When I encounter someone claiming to be an atheist, I ask questions about how they have reached their conclusion. During the conversation, I sometimes comment, "You and I certainly see this differently, but I admire your faith." The person usually rejects the possibility of having faith, but my genuine interest in their point of view often disarms them. A respectful response may assert that faith is required to believe we live in a universe that always existed or ultimately came from nothing, yet has amazing complexity based on an incalculable number of random changes. If the discussion environment has been positive, such a statement may stimulate continuing thoughts and interaction, even if initially rebuffed.

A distinct element of respectful, honest discussions designed to launch multipliers opens channels for the truth of Scripture to stimulate additional questions. That freedom helps a person explore dependence upon God's wisdom amid the issues shaping life. Learning to pursue a beneficial pattern while remaining sensitive to unexpected opportunities to explore other issues is absorbed by others through our example. The skills developed in such conversations will enrich any meaningful conversation, especially those with spiritual significance.

An Encouraging Thread

A few years ago, I unpacked a box of notes that had accumulated during four-plus decades of ministry. One hand-written card from Howard Hendricks, a beloved professor at Dallas Theological Seminary for six decades, was a special encouragement. While in seminary in Dallas, I spoke at a young adult retreat and mentioned some of the powerful truths I had learned from Dr. Hendricks's class on the Christian home. My host wrote him a well-deserved letter of thanks, which led to his note of special encouragement to me. "Prof," as his students affectionately called him, "listened" to a letter and kindly encouraged a student with only a marginal connection with him.

Prof modeled the *"affirmation, ask questions, give a helpful answer, and ask another question"* pattern in his classes, discipleship groups and individual conversations with profound effect. He and I enjoyed an encouraging friendship that was rooted in his close connection to the church I pastored in Fort Worth. But the influence of his life with thousands of students, pastors, missionaries, and parachurch leaders will mark the global church for decades to come. Millions of people taught and encouraged by thousands of local church pastors, media teachers like Chuck Swindoll, David Jeremiah, and Tony Evans, as well as parachurch ministries like Young Life,

Bible Study Fellowship, Cru (formerly Campus Crusade for Christ), Family Life, Walk Thru the Bible, and Search Ministries have been strengthened by the thread of honest, respectful conversations modeled and taught with enduring impact by Dr. Hendricks. His expanding thread still grows.

6

COMMUNICATING HISTORY'S
MOST AMAZING MESSAGE

The message entrusted to Christ's followers over two thousand years ago remains simple, unique, and powerful. The Gospel is *simple* enough that a child can grasp its reality and receive by faith the gracious offer of salvation made possible by Christ's sacrificial death on the cross. It remains *unique* as the only spiritual teaching that offers a Savior who completely paid the penalty for human sin so that salvation can be received and experienced as a gift from God. This truth alone presents a stark contrast with all other religious systems, which require human merit to gain God's favor, implicitly minimizing the awful reality of human sin. The Good News is so *powerful* that any person, no matter how sinful, who embraces Christ's gift by faith, can receive eternal life. This promise of eternal life offers security as God's children remain anchored in the faithfulness of the Father, not their performance. It also promises the Father's effective and loving discipline for all believers and initiates the privilege of serving Him daily.

Faithful, grateful witnesses of God's grace embrace the simplicity, uniqueness, and power of the Gospel, prompting worship in this life and forever. Discipleship leverages a believer's capacity to *explain* this message with clarity, gentleness, and respect while *embracing* the daily privilege of fruitful ministry that is prepared by God and motivates us to be grateful toward Him.

A Simple Message

God's message of salvation, that is revealed in the Bible, communicates the purpose of humanity while defining the tragic consequences of our sinful rebellion against Him. Our inability to remedy our desperate condition echoes throughout human history. The human problem of sin requires a divine solution that is provided in the person and work of Jesus Christ. The good news is that the solution is a gift that must be personally received by faith (Acts 16:31; Ephesians 2:8-9) with full confidence in the complete sufficiency of Christ's payment for sin. This results in forgiveness of sin and eternal life the moment we trust Christ (John 5:24; 1 John 5:11-13). We maximize this eternal relationship daily by obedient dependence upon God's empowerment through His indwelling Spirit. This simple message is communicated in five concepts:

1. **Good News**: People have a blessed **purpose**, created in God's image for intimate fellowship with Him as His steward, servant, and companion in this life and eternity (Genesis 1:26-27, 2:15- 25; 2 Corinthians 5:1-5).
2. **Bad News**: People have a devastating **problem** as sinners, which can derail their purpose in this life or eternity (Romans 6:23; Ephesians 2:1-3).
3. **Bad News Gets Worse**: People cannot fix this awful problem through their moral, religious, or spiritual endeavors, making their situation **hopeless without Christ** (Romans 1-3, especially 3:23).
4. **Great News:** (The best news ever): Jesus **paid for our sins completely** so that God can give salvation as a gift (Romans 3:21-26; Ephesians 2:4-7).

5. **Urgent News**: This gift of God's forgiveness and eternal life is **received by faith alone** and begins the **privilege** of serving Him by faith in this life (John 3:16; Ephesians 2:8-10).

First, our *purpose as creatures made in God's image is to experience intimate fellowship with Him as faithful stewards of His creation*. This principle, established in the first chapters of the Bible (Genesis 1:26-27, 2:15-24), shapes the wisdom we need for all human relationships. Knowing we are made in the image of the triune God has foundational importance, especially in a world that is frantically searching for purpose and tragically confused about issues such as human dignity and sexuality. Although there are many aspects of the "fingerprints" of God in creation, one of the most persistent is the paradigm of *unity embracing diversity and unleashing creativity*. We see this in the revelation of the triune God, the creation of human beings, the institution of marriage, the function of the natural world, and the ministry of the body of Christ. Communication and creativity, as well as loving, helping, or blessing family and friends, even in frail and flawed ways, reflect our purpose as creatures made in God's image. Even those who reject God's existence or refuse His grace reveal His image in their hopeless pursuit of fulfillment in ways that are often destructive and ultimately disappointment. Created in God's image, only intimacy with Him provides enduring fulfillment for any person.

Though we have a joyful purpose, we have a *crippling problem*. Humanity's rebellion, which began in Eden, permeates a ripple effect with catastrophic consequences. God warned Adam that sin would result in death. The Bible describes three dimensions of this penalty for sin: spiritual, physical, and eternal. Adam and Eve immediately experienced death, or separation, from God spiritually. They tried to cover their sin with fig leaves, hide from God, and avoid their problem. An awareness of their nakedness exposed their separation from God. Finally, the sacrifice of an animal by God provided a gracious covering for their nakedness and sin (Genesis 3:1-21).

This spiritual separation, which God ultimately remedied in Christ, created a cascade of hurt and loss as each generation of human parents passed sinful rebellion to their children. Paul declared that we are dead in our sin and are children of wrath—a spiritual reality known as *inherited sin* (Ephesians 2:1-3). We see it in ourselves and other people, even in our delightful grandchildren. The consequences are frequently aggravating, sometimes devastating, but, in all cases, evidence of a universal human problem.

Other consequences of sin are inevitable. Adam and Eve lived long lives in their physical bodies before separation from the earthly body through physical death. Every funeral we attend is a reminder that Adam's sin started a death spiral, impacting each person. Our physical bodies die and return to dust. Before we complain, ponder Paul's teaching on Adam's sin, *imputed* (credited) to every person (resulting in physical death), as analogous to Christ's righteousness *imputed* by grace to those who trust Him for eternal life (Romans 5:12-21).

Every person will ultimately be judged by God. For believers in Christ, their sin has been paid for on the cross and their judgment at the bema seat[1] will focus on their service for Christ (1 Corinthians 3:5-4:7). For people who have not received eternal life through faith in Christ, their judgment will include eternal condemnation—or separation from God. First, it will be confirmed that these people are not found in the Book of Life, which contains the names of all who have eternal life in Christ through faith. Then they will be judged according to their actions found in the book of deeds. Because the standard will be God's perfect righteousness, they will be eternally separated from God because of their *individual sin* (Revelation 20:10-15). This sobering truth should motivate all believers to share the Gospel with urgency and humility before God.

Our problem with sin is deeper and more devastating than we realize. Throughout history, people have attempted to bridge the chasm with God through good works, religious activities, or human accomplishments. One dramatic Old Testament example of such a futile attempt is the story of the Tower of Babel (Genesis 11:1-9). All human efforts to find favor with God or avoid the consequences of rebellion against Him eventually have catastrophic results.

Paul, the apostle to the Gentiles and a man of substantial religious and academic success (Acts 22:3; Philippians 3:4-7), concluded that we all "fall short of God's glory" (Romans 3:23). This does not mean we are as sinful as someone else or as bad as we could be, but when God sees our actions, thoughts, and motives, the sinful rebellion of every person is confirmed. No one can have a right relationship with God on their own terms. Both our sinfulness and inability to remedy our problems are central elements when communicating the Gospel with clarity to a culture that minimizes God's holiness and perversely exalts human goodness. A soft universalism, or "everyone goes to heaven if there is one," has become the dominant religious perspective in our world. The spiritual desperation that results from sin for each person is the biblical reality that necessitates God's provision of forgiveness and eternal life in Christ (Romans 1:18-3:20).

A Unique Message

Many religions acknowledge the elements of human sinfulness, but their solution is anchored in religious, moral, or personal action, providing all or part of a remedy. If religion offers a solution, there are a host of options. If you are convinced you need a Savior, Jesus is the only person in history who has made a credible claim to remedy sin, making this simple message *unique* among all religious systems past and present. The salvation communicated in the Gospel is *in Christ alone, by grace alone,* and *through faith alone.*

Christ Alone

Paul's letter to the believers in Rome is the most extensive explanation of the Gospel in the Bible. He began with clarity about the person of Jesus Christ, a descendent of David, who was declared the Son of God by the resurrection (Romans 1:1-4). He is Jesus Christ our Lord, who left heaven, humbled Himself by assuming perfect humanity without diminishing His full deity though voluntarily choosing to relate to people without demonstrating all His attributes (Philippians 2:5-11). All things were created and are sustained by Christ (Colossians 1:16) and are under His authority, power, and dominion (Ephesians 1: 20-22). The gospel message affirms Jesus's deity, humanity, and absolute authority woven into the lengthy (Romans 1-8) and brief presentations of this gracious truth.[2] Clarity about Jesus, God in the flesh, the King of Kings, and Lord of Lords (1 Timothy 6:15) strengthens humility before Him and confidence in the sufficiency of His work on the cross.

Our awful problem with sin can only be remedied by Jesus Christ, flawless in His obedience, fulfilling the Law in all regards (Matthew 5:17; Hebrews 4:15), and completely faithful in His mission to seek and save the lost (Mark 10:45; Luke 19:10). Christ's death satisfied God's wrath, providing redemption for sin, and demonstrating God's righteousness as just and that He is the justifier of all who have faith in Christ (Romans 3:24-26; Galatians 4:5). Jesus is the sole basis for our salvation (Matthew 20:28; 2 Corinthians 5:21), providing for the forgiveness and cleansing of our sins (1 John 1:5-2:2) and the blessings of reconciliation with God (Romans 5:1–5). His death provided a once and for all payment for sin, eliminating the need for additional sacrifices (Hebrews 7:27, 9:12, 27-28, 10:1-18). Like His identity as God's Son, the sufficiency of Christ's payment for sin is anchored in the reality of His resurrection (1 Corinthians 15:1-19).

15:50-58), and the certainty of judgment for all people (John 5:28-29; Acts 17:31).

The opponents of Jesus could not find his body. There have been only a few possible explanations offered: The disciples went to the wrong tomb; Romans and/or Jews took the body; the disciples took Jesus's body and perpetrated a massive hoax; Jesus did not die, only swooned (possibly drugged) and awakened, then removed the stone that sealed the tomb, overcame guards, saw disciples, and left Israel; or disciples hallucinated as a group (not medically possible, only an individual experience). All these explanations require significant faith, even more than believing Jesus was raised from the dead, ascended to heaven, and, through His followers, changed the world empowered by the Holy Spirit.[6]

This unique plan in Christ alone, by grace alone, and through faith alone, has stimulated controversy from the days of the apostles. The Galatians compromised the clarity of Paul's message by teaching that believers must embrace Jewish practices, prompting the apostle's scathing rebuke in his Galatians letter (1:5-9). Some teachers influenced by Greek philosophy taught gnostic concepts that distorted Jesus's person. The apostle John responds by emphasizing both Jesus's deity (John 1:1-5; 1 John 2:22-23) and humanity (John 1:14; 1 John 1:1-2). The book of Hebrews, distinctive because the author is not identified, begins with a vigorous affirmation of the person and work of Christ (Hebrews 1:1-4). This letter sustains an emphasis on the sufficiency of Jesus Christ's "once for all" sacrifice for sin (Hebrews 7:27, 9:12, 10:10) and declares it is impossible to please God without faith (Hebrews 11:1-6). The Bible addresses the confusion and controversy about our salvation regarding issues that affect each new generation of believers.

As believers explain this message to friends and acquaintances in casual encounters while pastors and evangelists explain this truth in group settings, the scope of interaction about Jesus's person and work will differ for each person. In a brief or lengthy explanation of the gospel message (Acts 16:31, 17:22-32), our hope rests on a God who is always working (John 5:17) before and during the conversation. He has a complete awareness of a person's heart and is powerful enough to finish the good work He starts with a first step of faith in this unique message of salvation in Christ (Philippians 1:6).

A Powerful Message

The concern about people who make false professions but are not followers of Christ is acknowledged in Scripture (Matthew 7:21-23; Luke 13:25-27).[7] Such people may be impressive religiously and fool others or even themselves, but God is never confused about who belongs to Him (Romans 8:29-30; 2 Timothy 2:19). Scripture also addresses the reality that sinful believers can be snared by fleshly disobedience when they do not experience God's empowerment by faith (Romans 7:14-23; 1 Corinthians 3:1-3). The letters that were written to believers in the first century are laced with admonitions, addressing disobedience within Christian communities and exhorting humility, confession, and restoration.[8] False teaching about the Gospel is boldly confronted (Galatians 1:5-9; 2 Peter 2:1-22; Jude 5-9) while simply communicating this life-changing message is a defining value for Christ's ambassadors (Acts 2:22-41, 7:2-60, 17:24-34, 26:1-29).

God's gracious salvation—received by faith—is secured and sustained by His power at work in us, which raised Jesus from the grave (Ephesians 1:19). There are three primary aspects of our salvation where this power is demonstrated: a believer's security in Christ, effective discipline by the Father, and the joyful blessing of being God's instrument in fruitful ministry.

The Security of the Believer

The security of a believer is anchored in Jesus's promise that those who belong to Him by faith cannot be snatched from Him or His Father (John 10:28-29). It would have been enough for Jesus to hold us in His hands. As God's Son and Sovereign King over all creation, Jesus has *infinite power* (Hebrews 1:3) But He adds that His Father who is *greater than all* also has each believer in His hands. Paul emphasized that those who belong to Christ are sealed by the indwelling Holy Spirit until the day of redemption (Ephesians 1:13-14, 4:30), signifying both their security and authenticity, validating that nothing can separate a believer from the Father's love (Romans 8:38-39). A believer's personal security and experiential assurance rests on the faithfulness of the triune God, confident the Father knows His children (2 Timothy 2:19), the Son loses none that the Father gives Him (John 6:37-39), and the Spirit bears inward witness that the believer belongs to God (Romans 8:15-16).

The believer's assurance of security in Christ is anchored in God's faithfulness to His promises. When a believer's past, present, or future faithfulness is the focus, uncertainty about salvation that brings doubt and discouragement is not surprising. When a person that you are discipling faces this confusing situation, there is an opportunity for you to clarify the scope and sufficiency of the Gospel. As you explore what Jesus did for the person on the cross, not what the person has done for Jesus, the message they once heard and believed can be reaffirmed.

Adding anything that a person must do beyond receiving God's grace by faith only weakens the person's genuine trust in the power of God to save and provide. Whether a preemptive commitment to cease disobedience to God in a specific area, the embrace of a religious ritual, or the pursuit of a particular pattern of spiritual discipline, any human activity added to trusting the person of Christ and His work on the cross for our salvation distorts what Paul explicitly affirmed (Ephesians 2:8-10) and suggests what he vigorously rejected (Galatians 1:6-9, 3:10-14). Security is anchored in the post-conversion reality of being God's child, not a pre-conversion clarity about the multi-faceted significance of Christ's Lordship.

The Father's Discipline of His Children

Secure believers rest in the knowledge that God is faithful to *discipline His children* (Hebrews 12:4-11). God knows each of His children and has the compassion and capacity to do whatever is needed to discipline them when they disobey. This disobedience can be morally reprehensible or socially respectable. God knows our hearts and works in each believer. His motivation is always love, and His methods are always *wise and powerful* enough to effectively deal with His child in harmony with His commitment to conform the person to the image of His Son (Romans 8:29). Discipline of believers is not always obvious to others, but the certainty of God's love and the scope of His methods must be emphasized. In addition to spiritual turmoil, emotional pain, and physical distress (Psalm 32:1-5), God may use disease and even death in the discipline of believers (Psalm 32:3–4; 1 Corinthians 11:30), sometimes by supernatural means (Acts 5:1-11) and often in the community of believers (Matthew 18:15-18; 1 Corinthians 5:1-13; 2 Corinthians 2:6-8). Though Ananias and Sapphira died as disciplined believers, the church in Jerusalem, gripped by the fear of the Lord, expanded greatly amid increasing persecution (Acts 5:12-41). God's love is tender and tough, in harmony with His ability to fulfill His purpose in and through His children.

We respond to who He is and what He has done on the cross as we trust Christ. Grasping the broad implications of this concept of God's loving discipline, before receiving Christ by faith, is not the emphasis of Scripture. When the discussion devolves to questions about how soon, how much, and how a person obediently yields to Christ's Lordship as the basis for a believer's assurance of salvation, personal confusion, and spiritual division are not a surprise. Grateful obedience to Jesus Christ is the path of fruitful blessing and should be taught and modeled consistently. Foolish disobedience to Jesus Christ as the path of damaged relationships, diminished influence, and the certainty of painful discipline should be explained with sober clarity as a believer begins to follow Christ. There is nothing "easy" about disobedience, which squanders the blessings of being God's child.

Painful discipline by God is the primary means for stimulating agreement with Him, or confession, about our sin. The goal of God's correction is that the believer be restored through a full embrace of Christ's payment for sin, resulting in cleansing, forgiveness, and the restoration of fellowship with God (1 John 1:9). This change of perspective or direction shapes the blessings of genuine repentance.

When my brothers and I were kids, my dad would take us to buy groceries on Saturday mornings so my mom could relax while my baby sister napped. On one of those trips, I encountered a friend named Mack. He and I simultaneously noticed a display of tuna cans stacked in a pyramid. We instantly responded like normal eight-year-old boys, pondering how many cans we could remove without the display collapsing. After removing just a few, a loud crash echoed through the store. The stock boy, store owner, and my friend's mom reacted in a predictable, dramatic fashion. My dad quietly walked over to me, painfully pinched my shoulder, and whispered, "We will deal with this when we get home." After a few minutes close to his side, we drove home—me still traumatized by his words. In a desperate attempt to deflect attention, I said, "Mack did it, too, and you are not upset with him." Without even glancing at me, he sternly said, "Mack is not my son." The painful, effective consequences awaiting at home, delivered convincingly by a loving though imperfect dad, affirmed my identity as his son. In a short while, I began to discover how the perfect heavenly Father effectively disciplines all of His children as He conforms them to the image of His Son (Romans 8:29).

The Spirit's Daily Empowerment

God's power, revealed through the security and discipline of the believer, is an encouraging and sobering reality, but there is also a personal blessing that expresses God's power in our daily lives in ways that touch eternity. Our eternal salvation in Christ by grace through faith offers this great privilege. Paul's letter to the Colossians declares, "just as you received Christ Jesus as Lord, continue to live in him" (Colossians 2:6). We begin living with Christ by grace through faith, and we live in Him by grace through faith (Galatians 2:20). The letter to the Hebrews declares "without faith, it is impossible to please God" (Hebrews 11:6). Believers are carefully crafted in Christ, for good works, prepared by God beforehand (Ephesians 2:10).

Believers are not saved by works but are empowered by the Spirit (Ephesians 1:19, 5:18) to enjoy the blessing of being part of the work God plans for them. Sounds like a *daily celebration of "in Christ by grace through faith,"* revealing God's power while filling the believer with the joy that is promised to those abiding in Christ and bearing fruit (John 15:1-11). The next chapter explores this privilege with such joyful blessings.

In April 1960, not long after the tuna can episode, my eight-year-old heart struggled with turmoil. I had gotten tangled in some bad behavior, making my sinfulness a persistent distress that was amplified by the possibility that my parents would hear about my foolishness. In an evangelistic meeting, the guest preacher explained the Gospel simply enough for me to grasp both the present and eternal consequences of my sinfulness and the amazing offer of forgiveness and eternal life possible only through Christ's death on the cross. The urgency for me to personally accept that gift through faith in Christ's payment became clear. I followed the preacher in a simple prayer, acknowledging my sinfulness and accepting God's salvation. It felt like a massive burden lifted from my life.

Almost ten years later, I began to understand the patterns and perspectives that would help me more consistently enjoy the gift I received as a child. I made many commitments to God, failed frequently, and cultivated an exterior spirituality that was more about impressing others than pleasing God. Occasional flashes of intimacy with God intertwined with frequent, discouraging attempts to keep my life respectable. Yet, I had no confusion about being God's child, tenderly nurtured, convincingly disciplined, and patiently encouraged as I limped forward in my walk with Christ. Struggling often, I was alive to God and aware of the light of His Word (Colossians 1:12-13, 2:13-14), even if I was frequently disobedient to it. My hope for heaven persisted, in part, because someone had told me that God, like my dad, would be faithful to discipline His children (Psalm 32:1-5; Hebrews 12:4-11). My concern was not going to heaven, but how I would survive spiritually in the college years ahead.

The struggle with fleshly desires that Paul illustrated in his own life (Romans 7:15-25) and declared to be a universal reality became personal and painful: depending on myself would never provide the fulfillment for which God created me. Even as I experienced the spiritual turmoil and fleshly stresses described by Paul (Romans 7:14-25; 1 Corinthians 3:1-3), God demonstrated His faithfulness as He worked in moments of grateful obedience. This taste of God's power in transforming life stirred a spiritual appetite that I did not yet clearly understand. As I graduated from high school and went to Mississippi to be a counselor at a youth camp, God began to help me take the first steps in grasping biblical truths, yielding freedom and fruitfulness. Part of God's preparation was an awareness that I desperately needed His help to minister to the students at the camp. When I sought His help, He worked (John 5:17), revealing His grace and power. It was a meaningful step toward living by faith just as I had been given salvation by faith years before (Colossians 2:6-7).

An Encouraging Thread

The message about Jesus as the Savior of the world spread rapidly in the centuries following His death and resurrection. Confusion about both His person as the perfect God-man and His work as the sacrificial substitute to pay the penalty for human sin provoked theological conflict. Three pivotal leaders in the fourth and fifth centuries held like a strong rope to the core truths about Jesus. Athanasius, Ambrose, and Augustine served God, and their connections remind us that God is always at work.

Athanasius became the bishop of Alexandria (296-373) after the condemnation of the teaching of Arius at the Council of Nicaea in 325. Arius denied the deity of Christ by claiming that Jesus was created before time and God alone was divine. A gifted speaker, who utilized musical tunes to enlarge his heretical influence, Arius prompted decades of turmoil as Roman emperors weighed in with their differing views. Athanasius was exiled five times, spending years in a monastic lifestyle while writing about his views. He was an uncompromising advocate for Jesus as fully God, who in the incarnation became a perfect man, so that, through his death, sinful people could be redeemed. Amid this theological tumult, Athanasius promoted monastic disciplines, emphasized the devotional use of the Psalms, and became the first to affirm the twenty-seven books we now know as the New Testament in 367.[9] His writings and example prevailed, and Arius' views eventually subsided.

Ambrose (339-397) was the provincial governor of Milan. His political responsibilities and personal views made the Arian controversy significant. A convinced follower of Athanasius, Ambrose attended in his political role when the church leaders in Milan gathered in 373 to replace the deceased bishop who had followed Arius. When he spoke to calm the crowd, they chose him as bishop by acclamation. Ambrose led with exceptional credibility.[10]

Ambrose relinquished his political position and became a bishop who championed the Athanasian view of Christ as fully God and perfect man, finally affirmed conclusively at Chalcedon in 451. Ambrose provided pivotal leadership toward this positive outcome. Ambrose also introduced hymn singing in worship gatherings, being credited with writing four hymns. He revealed great courage when he convinced Emperor Theodosius, who had supported Christianity, to publicly apologize for the massacre of 7,000 civilians in Thessalonica because they rioted against an imperial decree. This bold leadership enhanced Ambrose's influence beyond Milan.[11]

A gifted communicator, Ambrose impressed a young teacher of rhetoric in Milan. Born in north Africa, and raised by a devout Christian mother, Augustine (354-430) vacillated between religious asceticism and licentious living in Africa and after moving to Milan. He struggled spiritually until Ambrose's teaching and example led him to faith in Christ in 387. Ambrose's Athanasian clarity about the person of Christ contributed to Augustine's passionate emphasis on the work of Christ for our salvation, making Augustine perhaps the most influential theologian in the history of the church. Augustine contended with Pelagius, who denied that a sinful nature inherited from Adam eliminated a person's capacity to please God. Augustine strongly affirmed the sinfulness of mankind, making each person incapable of pleasing God without salvation in Christ.[12]

The growing consolidation of the religious and political power in Rome made a choice between these opposing theologies inevitable. The eventual affirmation of the Pelagian view fueled an expanding sacramental system that was ultimately crafted with economic precision by Peter Lombard in the eleventh century,[13] established officially by the Fourth Lateran Council in 1215, and affirmed by the master theologian Aquinas in the thirteenth century.[14]

This transactional matrix of rituals experienced in a language unknown to the common people claimed to dispense the "merited grace" that was deemed essential for hope beyond this life. These sacraments understandably became the central priority for the religious life of priests and people. This system, asserting control over a person's eternal destiny, led to institutional corruption and spiritual despair. When Reformation leaders pondered the history of the church, it was the writings of Augustine,[15] Ambrose's protégé, which gave them a theological foundation for the message of salvation in Christ alone, by grace alone, through faith alone—a thread precious beyond measure.

7

EMBRACING LIFE'S MOST AWESOME PRIVILEGE

I served as a Christian camp counselor for two months the summer before beginning college. After several weeks, the physical exhaustion and spiritual refreshment from that experience created a fresh openness to pivotal growth in my walk with Christ. Daily biblical teaching, friendships with dynamic counselors, and awareness that God was working in the ministry with teenage campers fueled my short-term encouragement. My concern centered on how that kind of life could become a consistent pattern when the highly structured camp environment morphed into the stresses of school and relationships at college.

On June 26, 1969, a camp speaker taught about living each day with intentional dependence on God's Spirit.[1] Though I had memorized verses about trusting God, abiding in Christ, and walking by faith (Proverbs 3:5-6; John 15:4-5; Galatians 5:16), I had gained little conceptual "Velcro" to help me obey these verses consistently. The speaker unpacked truths about presenting our lives to God, not only as an act of dedication but as a daily declaration of dependence on the empowerment of God's Spirit (Romans 6:1-4; Romans 12:1-2; Ephesians 5:15-18). My surprise at hearing this teaching probably revealed evidence of my failure to hear what others had attempted to teach me. Certain of salvation for eternity by grace alone through faith alone, I perceived the Christian life as giving my best effort to validate being worthy of such a gift.

This confused but common perspective led to anxiety, anger at myself and others, and occasional arrogance when others noticed and applauded my efforts. As I pondered his encouraging message, I made a decisive pivot, counting myself dead to sin but alive to God based on a new understanding of my identity as God's child in Christ. I began a long journey of learning how to experience this newness of life through a persistent presentation of my life to God as a grateful servant.

A few months later, my involvement with Campus Crusade at Auburn University helped me discover how the truth I heard at camp provided the foundation for a life committed to intentional evangelism and discipleship. *Cru* (as it is now known) had a little blue booklet that explained the concepts I had heard at camp. During those years, I learned the basics of living by faith, experiencing a sometimes-stumbling measure of the blessing of dependence on the Spirit's power day by day. But the decades since have been an ongoing process of discovering, through my growth and struggles, ways to help believers daily embrace this privilege. This chapter will explore the concepts at the heart of fruitful, joyful ministry, especially for people preparing spiritual multipliers.

One of the most striking concepts in the Bible declares that it is impossible to please God without faith (Hebrews 11:6). Not faith in faith, but faith in God for forgiveness and life everlasting, as well as for the daily empowerment needed to be God's co-laborer. Considering this provocative, absolute statement, it is appropriate to explore how living by faith can be consistently experienced by a grateful believer.

Discovering Transformational Truths

There is an aspect of our relationship with God that we must grasp before we can consistently live by faith. Through the example of Abraham and David, the apostle Paul demonstrated that believers are justified, or declared righteous, by faith (Romans 4:1-24). This profound act of grace not only changes our standing before God, but it also permanently roots our core identity in Christ as we receive the righteousness of God through faith (Romans 5:12-21; Philippians 3:9). This new identity provides the basis for experiencing the privilege that God desires for each of His children.

In Romans 6:1-11, Paul addresses a provocative question about continuing to sin so that grace will increase: *Shall I continue in sin so that grace can abound?* The question, rooted in the confusion spawned by Satan's constant lies, disregards the tragic relational damage of sin (Galatians 5:19-21). It forgets the certainty of a loving Father's painful discipline (Hebrews 12:4-11) and the squandering of our opportunity to live now in ways rewarded for eternity (Ephesians 5:15-17; 1 Timothy 6:17-19).

Not surprisingly, Paul's response begins with a righteous expletive that is translated, "May it never be!" His answer explains that grace is providing freedom from sin's domination, not freedom to continue sinning. He roots this response in a new identity that is gained the moment we trust Christ for salvation. This new identity is rooted in our shared spiritual experience in Christ's crucifixion, burial, and resurrection to live a new life by God's grace through faith day by day. It *triggers the spiritual transformation* that God ultimately accomplishes for His children. It does not mean we are not capable of sin, but we are no longer compelled to sin by our flesh, nor able to continue in sin without being disciplined by God the Father. Sin may give momentary exhilaration, but mounting exhaustion and exasperation are inevitable for God's child (Psalm 32:1-5).

Our union with Christ through faith releases us from slavery to sin and provides us with a new life in Christ. These blessings, anchored in this new identity, can only shape our daily life through the Spirit's power. Pursuing patterns to strengthen our union with Christ, described as abiding in Him, guides our prayer life, glorifies the Father, fuels fruitful ministry, motivates our love toward Christ, and enlarges our joy (John 15:1-11). Having described this new life as union with Christ, Paul issued the first command in his letter to the Romans as the catalyst for the privilege of being God's instrument. The command, translating a word from which we get the English term *logic,* means *to consider, or count.*[2] Paul presented this new reality as the defining perspective for a believer: *dead to sin and alive to God.* Placing this new identity as the starting point and guiding pattern becomes essential for the person who enjoys a new life as a believer. This is the asset column contrasted with the debit column of fleshly slavery to sin. A decisive embrace of this new identity can only be experienced through daily dependence on God.

This pivotal command, which is explained in Romans 6:12–23, describes a *trajectory for spiritual transformation* defined by three issues. First, Paul correctly assumes that every person serves someone or something. In verses 12-14, who or what you serve is the issue. Paul's command to not allow sin to rule in our bodies is clarified by two more commands, putting the issue in terms of a binary choice: present your body to unrighteous sin, or present yourself as a person who is alive from the dead as God's instrument of righteousness. These commands assume that believers can make the former choice with all its painful consequences. This reality heightens the urgency of obedience to the second command.

In Romans 6:15-18, Paul addressed *the test of spiritual transformation,* revealing how people can discern which master they are serving. In harmony with Jesus's teaching that you cannot serve two masters (Matthew 6:24), Paul rightly concluded that obedience reveals a person's master. Although we may fool others and even ourselves for a while, we never fool God. The identity of our master will eventually be revealed in our lives.

Paul gave specific instructions to believers on how to live a life with Christ as your master. First, a follower must *persistently focus on Christ, especially His death on the cross* to provide full payment for sin and complete satisfaction of God's wrath, clarifying the awfulness of our sin and amplifying gratitude toward Christ. Paul summarized the theological foundation in Romans 3:21-6:23 with his exhortation to the Corinthians, "For I determined to know nothing among you except Jesus Christ, and him crucified" (1 Corinthians 2:2). This perspective cultivates an attitude toward sin that is rooted in the reality that each disobedient choice required Jesus's death on the cross. This jarring truth helps a believer remain on the path of obedient dependence on God's Spirit. Sin always reflects Satan's lies, which began in Eden and are most revealed in Jesus's temptation in the wilderness (Matthew 4:1-11). In both His payment for our sin and example of rejecting temptation with God's truth, Jesus provides the way of freedom from bondage to sin (Romans 7:25). The night before His crucifixion, Jesus exhorted is apostles to abide, or dwell, in Him (John 15:1-11). As a believer keeps the focus on Jesus while depending on His strength in prayer, the blessing is both fruitfulness and joy that are possible through obedience to the Master.

Every believer can relate to dealing with sin when ensnared by fleshly impulses (Romans 7:13-24) or provoked by Satan's lies (John 8:44). Scripture emphasizes a second truth that is essential for a wise response: *face your sin honestly.* Confessing our sin to God (1 John 1:9) is not a "drive-through" transaction where we mechanically admit we did something sinful and thank God that Jesus paid for it on the Cross. To see sin the way God does, we must linger at the Cross (1 Corinthians 2:2), considering the specific sin that required the death of Christ, and embracing God's perspective about our sin as thoroughly as possible.

This agreement with God changes our thoughts about our sins, stimulates gratitude for Christ's death as payment for the specific sin, and guides a new path of obedience, reflecting a change of mind, heart, and direction. This transformed perspective that guides obedient living reflects biblical repentance. *Genuine agreement with God about our sin (confession) opens the door to invigorating repentance as we walk by faith.* As our view of sin becomes more consistent with God's truth, following Paul's example as we discipline our body and make it our slave (1 Corinthians 9:27), by presenting our bodies as "a living and holy sacrifice" (Romans 12:1), we reap the fruit of transformed minds. Such an obedient life is motivated by pleasing the One with whom we are united in His crucifixion, resurrection, and new life (Romans 6:1-10).[3]

Believers are in a war zone against spiritual forces, but our strength is rooted in what Christ did for us when He nailed the debt we owed to the Cross (Colossians 2:14), and our help is discovered in humbly drawing near to God (James 4:7-10). As we put on God's armor (Ephesians 6:12-20), reflecting His provision for the spiritual battles of life, we are prepared to resist sinful pressures in a world seeking to squeeze us in ways that displease God and disrupt His blessings for believers. The fight is not ultimately between the believer and sinful enticement but between God and the spiritual forces opposing Him. Submit to God, draw near to Him, clothed in His armor, and Satan must flee. Christ's victory over sin is our sustaining hope (Romans 7:25).

A third biblical truth critical for a life of spiritual freedom and fruitfulness is the urgency to immediately *flee temptation, avoiding situations where we are vulnerable to sin.* (1 Corinthians 6:18; 1 Timothy 6:10-11; 2 Timothy 2:22). When we make choices that invite fleshly pressures, it should not be surprising that we stumble into sinful disobedience. Paul assured his readers that there is no temptation where God is not faithful to provide a way of escape (1 Corinthians 10:13). Because Jesus never sinned, it is reasonable that He knows temptation completely in both practical and spiritual terms. This brings us back to persistent focus on Christ. He provides for our forgiveness and offers perfect wisdom as we flee temptation in ways that enable us to live in grateful obedience.

Believers have different vulnerabilities to situations that inflame fleshly desires: social prestige, physical pleasure, abundant possessions, and relational power. As we give no opportunity to fleshly desires (Romans 13:14) and proactively affirm our identity with Christ in His crucifixion for our sin (Romans 8:13), we can look consistently for the good works God has prepared for us (Ephesians

2:10). The joy of fruitful ministry provides an enduring protection against vexing temptation, just as healthy grass gives weeds no room in a beautiful lawn.

There is helpful accountability with other believers as spiritual struggles are faced (1 Corinthians 5:1-5; 1 Thessalonians 5:14-15). In an era when addiction to substances and sinful behaviors are rampant, churches often have ministries designed to provide counsel and support for people struggling with sinful behaviors. Many have found God's help in those settings; however, no amount of relational accountability can compensate for an unwillingness to focus on Christ, face your sin, and flee temptation with sober awareness that waiting to fight the approaching temptation is perilous.

During my time in Fort Worth, our church hosted J. Oswald Sanders as a guest speaker. He was a global missionary leader, a prolific author (including books like *Spiritual Leadership* and *Enjoying Intimacy with God*), and a master encourager in his eighties at the time. He requested a brief meal and rest on Saturday evening after he arrived, and I was given the privilege of that time with him. He was weary, but our conversation reflected his desire to encourage a young pastor. After the meal, I took him to his hotel. To my surprise, he asked me to come to his room for prayer.

After we put his luggage in a corner, we knelt beside the bed and he nodded to me to begin. I prayed with gratitude for our conversation and expectation for the ministry that would unfold the following day. When I stopped, he poured his heart out to God. After several minutes of being focused on God's goodness to him and Christ's provision of forgiveness for his sin, he began to unpack his need for God's strength and help as he faced the challenges of travel and the pressures of ministry. He acknowledged the temptation to seek to please people as well as other areas of struggle and asked God to protect him and empower him the following day. As he prayed, I thought, "You mean, I will continue to have these issues fifty years from now?" As he concluded his prayer, I realized I was with a man who knew and served his Master. Oswald Sanders is with Jesus now. Almost forty years later, his prayer illustrates the path of "counting yourself dead to sin, but alive to God" (Romans 6:11).

Even when a person begins with intentional dependence on God's power to be His instrument, it may be possible to stumble into sin by drifting to a selfish focus. Restoration of fellowship with God through confession of sin is essential (1 John 1:9). Honesty about your life initiates the steps toward renewing the blessings of new life in Christ. Fortunately, God desires to help you see your life clearly (Psalm 139:23-24).

Paul emphasized clarity about the outcome of sin and righteousness. Sin has destructive consequences in this life for any person, and it results in eternal separation from God for those who have not received God's righteousness through faith in Christ. For the believer destined for eternal life through Christ, clarity about sin's destructiveness should strengthen obedience to the pivotal command, "Count yourself dead to sin, but alive to God" (Romans 6:11). This foundational perspective unleashes the privilege of daily partnership with God, which amplifies the blessing of being His instrument in the good works prepared for every believer. The remainder of the letter to the Roman church unpacks the challenge summarized by these commands as well as the supernatural power available through faith that is essential for consistent obedience.

Doubling Down on Dependence on God

Faith is required to please God. We trust Christ for an eternal relationship with God by faith, and we live as God's instrument of righteousness each day by faith (Colossians 2:6-7). Because we cannot please God without faith, understanding how we experience faith in our lives as followers of Christ becomes essential. Framing this priority as a three-step process adds practical insights for a posture of dependence on God:

1. Embrace Faith
2. Envision Obedience
3. Expect Empowerment

A person *embraces faith* when "faith that pleases God chooses to know and obey God's Word regardless of feelings, circumstances, or cultural pressures" is a defining, daily reality, a "front-burner" issue in a person's life.[4] Obedience to God's Word as evidence of faith in God in a specific situation anchors this principle.

When we disobey, we declare our feelings, circumstances, or cultural values have greater significance for us than God's wisdom. As one of my early partners in multiplication affirmed, "It is like saying, 'I am smarter than God.'" The faith principle persistently pushes us toward honesty and helps us see theoretical agreement or good intentions that should never be confused with obedient faith (James 1:22-25). Summarized by the phrase *embrace faith, this* signifies a persistent, honest desire to please God through humble, grateful obedience.

With this sobering truth consistently before us, the importance of knowing what God's Word teaches becomes an urgent matter. As we examine Scripture, a persistent question must be this: If I live today in obedience to this biblical truth, how will my life be different? *Envision obedience* describes this critical step. The need for being specific in this decisive aspect of living by faith becomes obvious. Once we see a biblical truth we have not obeyed, we must identify instances of disobedience, confess those transgressions to the Lord, and pray and plan for specific obedience in the future.

Like athletes in many sports, our high school football team watched the film of our previous game to see ways that we could improve. As the film clicked forward, the coaches would affirm positive plays and expose the reasons some plays failed, often a painful but necessary step toward improvement. The practices helped players learn how to perform properly in similar situations in the next game. It involved a two-step process: (1) see the mistake clearly and (2) prepare intentionally for the next opportunity. When we envision obedience, we need to be very specific about our sin, agree with God fully about it, and seek wisdom about what obedience looks like. We need God's power to obey, but clarity about both our sin and opportunity for obedience will help us see our next "play" as it approaches.

One of my multiplication partners had been married a couple of years when we started meeting. As we discussed envisioning obedience, I asked him how consistently he loved his wife as the Bible commands. Still, in the afterglow of his honeymoon season, he affirmed the consistency of his love. I asked if his wife occasionally did not feel loved even if she knew he loved her. He processed the question and finally said, "Well, when I sleep late after she goes to work, then have to study in the evening when she comes home, she does not feel loved." This launched a fruitful conversation about what love looked like in his wife's eyes. This insight helped him envision obedience to God in terms of studying in the morning so he could have some flexibility for time with his wife in the evening. He knew what he should do, but he still needed a final element of the faith process to experience the changes needed to bless his marriage.

The final step affirms a posture of confident dependence on God's power as we obey with a grateful heart. Jesus stated, "It is to your advantage that I go away; for if I do not go away, the Helper will not come to you; but if I go, I will send Him to you" (John 16:7). With these stunning words, hours before His crucifixion, Jesus affirmed the disciples, and all of His followers in the centuries since have an advantage with the Holy Spirit in them over the disciples who shared years in Jesus's physical presence.

One of the key leaders among the disciples, a fisherman named Peter, explained how God's power provides everything we need to live a life pleasing to God (2 Peter 1:3). Peter doubled down in the next verse, declaring followers of Jesus would become partakers of the divine nature in response to God's promises. These revolutionary concepts are foundational for a person who desires to consistently enjoy the privilege of dependence on God. The apostle Paul exhorted his readers to keep in step with the Spirit and be controlled by the Spirit (Galatians 5:25; Ephesians 5:18). If this final step in the faith process became a bumper sticker, it would be *Expect Empowerment.* Having first understood this principle the summer before I started college, it took years of faltering personal experience, yielding both fruitful ministry and discouraging distraction, to gain greater clarity about how such empowerment can be embraced.

Strengthening an Intentional Posture

These concepts, initially formed in a personal walk with Christ and clarified through the teaching ministry in a local church, reflect the benefits of numerous conversations with faithful people who were personally discovering both the challenges and blessings of consistently depending on God's empowerment. The following chart reflects their questions and insights.

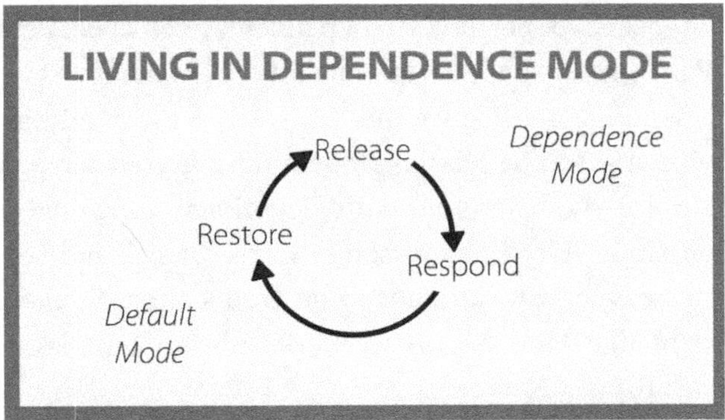

This diagram shows a daily pattern for a person who desires a consistent partnership with God. This three-stage process consists of two primary operational outcomes: *Dependence Mode* or *Default Mode*. Dependence mode entails an intentional posture of relying on God's power to please Him. Living in dependence mode requires persistent intentionality and supernatural help. Default mode needs neither of these. It is how people normally operate in life because, from our earliest moments, we have been refining our instincts to do what satisfies our selfish desires. As noted earlier, raising children and encouraging grandchildren confirms no one must be taught to be selfish, hurtful, or dishonest. Children grab, hit, and lie and must be taught by example, instruction, and discipline to share, be kind, and tell the truth. Although we may become more sophisticated in how we express and rationalize sinful behaviors, we never lose our vulnerability to these patterns.

Embracing Dependence Mode

Three steps help a believer spend an increasing part of the day experiencing the blessings of dependence mode. First, at the beginning of your day, as an act of worship (Romans 12:1–2), consciously *release* the control of your life to God's Spirit. This daily pattern cultivates a decisive posture of dependent obedience commanded earlier in Paul's letter to the Roman believers (Romans 6:11–15). You can do this with the confidence that God will provide all the spiritual resources you need to be His instrument during your day (Ephesians 1:19; 2 Peter 1:3–4). After your daily devotional time, once you have reflected on God's Word, confessed any known sin, and shared time with God in prayer, you can depend on God's strength and enter the day confident that God has good works already prepared for you (Ephesians 2:10).

With your life presented to God, you are then ready to *respond* to specific situations fashioned by God in the relational context of your family, job, recreation, or other activities. As your day unfolds, you will begin to see opportunities enough to act in the moment and learn how to not regret a missed opportunity in the spiritual "rearview mirror." Each day becomes an exciting adventure where a focus on pleasing Christ increases our joy (John 15:11) as we spend more of our time in dependence mode during the appointments, activities, and interruptions of life.

Discerning Default Mode

As life unfolds, you will inevitably encounter situations where your selfish tendencies provoke behaviors that disrupt the privilege of serving God. It could be a sarcastic comment to a coworker, a lustful thought as you scroll social media, or an envious attitude toward a neighbor. The fleshly nature hinders a believer's ability to stay in step with the Spirit. You have reverted to default mode, depending on yourself to satisfy what pleases you in the moment. Default mode is so challenging because it is the persistent setting in life. When we do not intentionally depend on God by faith, we soon resume reliance on ourselves. This prevalent pattern is a comfortable, normal feeling even though it ruins relationships and brings heartache to our lives.

This self-reliant posture, cultivated throughout our lives, is not always obvious. When a person's actions are sinful, believers have no confusion about the need to be *restored* by confession of the sin. But we sometimes assume that doing what God commands means full dependence on God will follow. Pursuing fruitful ministry can lead to a surprising, more intense, struggle with sin. Conversations with others in ministry indicate three frequent consequences when people attempt to minister to others but unwittingly rely on their strength.

First, they experience *anxiety*. When people attempt to serve God in their strength, anxiety becomes a common outcome. God did not create people to please Him in their flesh, but only through faith in Him. *Anxiety stimulates stress and sabotages joy.* Trying harder to accomplish God's purpose may impress others or give momentary validation to the person, but the anxiety usually increases. In a world filled with stresses, learning to dependently serve God in ways that defuse anxiety can be a huge blessing both personally and relationally.

Unresolved *anger* also indicates a person is in default mode. Anger becomes inevitable in life because it is the human response to hurt. Since we live in a world of hurts, we will get angry, sometimes during ministry opportunities.[5] The issue is whether we remain angry or follow God's path toward healing and restoration. Wisely and promptly addressing anger helps people continue in dependence on God (Ephesians 4:15, 26-27, 32). When anger takes root, relationships are damaged, and dependence on God's empowerment is compromised.

Finally, there are times when ministry endeavors have surprisingly fruitful outcomes. People who have been blessed will share their encouragement, and the person doing the ministry begins to look for ways to stimulate the applause. When well-intentioned affirmation is held close to a person's heart, a very short path leads to *arrogance*. Such arrogance indicates we perceive ourselves as the source of whatever we are doing. Arrogance can only be addressed with proactive humility (1 Peter 5:6-7). Like anger, humility is inevitable for the believer (Proverbs 3:34). If we humble ourselves, God will lift us up. If not, He will humble us.

Dealing with Fleshly Motivations

Anxiety, anger, and arrogance are leading indicators that a person is in a self-reliant posture, even if the actions of the believer are biblical. Any activity that is potentially helpful for spiritual growth or fruitful ministry can be pursued in the flesh (Matthew 6:1-18). It may be satisfying short-term and even impressive to others long-term, but it will not please God, and it cannot give the joy for which God created people. When we realize we are in this position, we do not need to wait until the next morning or Sunday for a fresh start. Confident in Christ as our righteous Advocate ready to stand with us, we wholeheartedly agree with God about our sin (1 John 1:7-2:2).

People who experience God's forgiveness that is provided in Christ are restored to fellowship with Him. This blessing is joyful, but it does not remove the temporal consequences of sin. Embracing this reality as an opportunity to trust God to graciously work through our lives will require enough time to see sin from God's perspective.

We may need wise counsel to pursue reconciliation with those we have wounded. Someone may not immediately forgive us. If so, we patiently wait for God to heal the hurt as we pray for His blessings on others. As we walk in humility, renewed with gratitude for His mercy and grace, we release control of our lives to God and eagerly look for ways to serve Him with people in the circumstances of our day. This *release/respond/restore* pattern will likely have to be repeated numerous times each day. It becomes a way to keep in step with the Spirit who empowers humble, available, and forgiven people.

Leveraging Interruptions to Strengthen Dependence on God

As believers live by faith, interruptions are inevitable and revealing. Whether a flat tire, a surprise visitor, or a broken appliance, each day will have unexpected events that disturb or derail our plans. Our hopes to finish the project or eat a quiet lunch are dashed by something or someone. For the person fixated on the tasks on the schedule, interruptions are often aggravations. For someone struggling to validate their competence, they can be an excuse. But for the person intentionally living in dependence mode as God's instrument, these are moments of possible spiritual opportunity.

Whether you are spending a few minutes in prayer and reflection as police untangle a traffic accident or encountering an unexpected individual in need (in person or on the phone), the possibility that God may have plans for the moment can bring both freedom and fruitfulness. Believers are not obligated to answer every call or help with every problem. Some calls need to be sent to voicemail, and some situations need to be addressed by others. But a person in dependence mode can be open to interruptions.

When the indwelling Spirit stirs an awareness that a situation may be part of God's good work, availability for at least a brief encounter will often bring surprising blessings. It may become clear that someone else is the person for the need and we wisely (and promptly) point them in the right direction. But sometimes we have been created for such a "good work." Some of God's best gifts are clothed as interruptions. Joyful people allow God to help them see such opportunities as they approach rather than through a glance in the rearview mirror.

Each day, believers in Christ have the privilege of intentional dependence on God's empowerment, bearing the fruit of love, joy, and peace, blessing relationships and ministry.[6] Daily confession of sin and focusing on Christ's sacrificial death stimulates gratitude for Christ and humility before God. When believers release their lives to God, respond to opportunities that God prepared, and promptly embrace the restoration of fellowship by confession and forgiveness, the opportunities to co-labor with God in ways that He has purposed for us will multiply.

Jesus told His apostles to abide in Him, pray, bear fruit, and be filled with joy (John 15:1-11). Paul unpacked this pattern in his letter to the church in Rome. It can be described as living in dependence mode, life's most awesome privilege for believers who live humbly before God and are fueled by gratitude for God's gift in Christ.

An Encouraging Thread

On the edges of the expanding Roman Empire, God continued working in the fourth through seventh centuries. He used three leaders who were connected by God's providence to change history —Patrick, Columba, and Aidan. Most people have heard of Patrick, but very few have heard of the other two. All contribute to a thread that encourages us to consistently depend on God, especially in the storms of life.

Patrick (389-461) grew up in a Christian home, probably in Roman Britain. Kidnapped at sixteen and taken as a slave to Ireland, Patrick labored as a shepherd for six years before escaping. During those years, Patrick's faith was strengthened. He returned home confident that he should return as a missionary to Ireland. A season in Gaul in western Europe exposed Patrick to monastic disciplines that shaped his ministry in Ireland, beginning in 432. Though not well educated, he emphasized spiritual disciplines and encouraged education. As more people trusted Christ, spiritual communities gathered around monasteries suited for the agrarian economy.[7] Patrick's contagious passion for missions and his Celtic converts led to the advancement of an evangelistic message throughout Europe. The message they taught emphasized orthodoxy and Trinitarian theology, affirming Christ's incarnation and sacrificial death for man's sin. Patrick's breastplate affirms a theological declaration centered on Christ, proclaiming His all-encompassing sufficiency.[8]

While our culture celebrates a wildly different perception of Patrick, the impact of his life advanced the gospel and enriched Europe spiritually and culturally through leaders like Columba and Aidan. Columba (521-597) grew up as an Irish nobleman and was educated in a school that reflected on Patrick's influence. After ordination, he took a pilgrimage with eleven associates and founded a monastery on the island of Iona.[9] It became a training center for missionaries, prioritizing the copying of the Scriptures and preaching the gospel. In the decades after Columba's death, Aiden received training at Iona.

The influence of the Celtic missionaries prompted King Oswald of Northumbria to invite Aidan to come to England. He founded a monastery in Lindisfarne through which King Oswald and many of his subjects responded to the gospel. From Lindisfarne, missionaries traveled to France and then to Switzerland and North Italy. The monasteries they developed became spiritual and intellectual beacons during what is often called "the dark ages." Some have argued that these faithful multipliers saved civilization because the monasteries helped preserve the spiritual and intellectual resources that shaped the environment in which the Reformation eventually flourished.[10] Certainly, their thread is one of the most significant in the tapestry of God's grace prevailing through faithful people.

8

CULTIVATING PATTERNS OF FAITHFUL MINISTRY

Paul's letter to the Philippians conveys a strong but loving exhortation on the blessings of relational unity among believers packaged in a personal "thank you" for years of generous support (Philippians 4:15–16). With gratitude to God for these friends and confidence God would complete His gracious work in believers, Paul illustrated, by example, a life of faith in Christ. He exhorted obedience on the path of spiritual unity with the humility modeled perfectly by Jesus Christ. He exhorted his readers to work out their salvation as God worked in them (Philippians 2:12-16). This short but powerful passage outlines specific ways that a believer can maximize the awesome privilege of being part of God's gracious purpose. Christ's ministry demonstrated that seeking and saving the lost as His urgent priority (Luke 19:10), and His commitment to building His church continues to this day (Matthew 16:18).

These enduring priorities are reflected in Paul's exhortation regarding the ways believers are blessed to be joint heirs with Christ as instruments, co-laborers, and servants who reflect God's gracious workmanship (1 Corinthians 3:9; 2 Corinthians 11:23; Ephesians 2:10). First, Paul presented this kind of blessing as the fruit of a persistent reliance on God's empowerment. The word translated *work out* relates to energy, and is a verb tense that indicates urgency and endurance. This urgent action embraces an engagement with God in which He empowers a proactive, obedient response in the unfolding circumstances of life. As we work out our eternal salvation through Christ in our daily life, we do so by faith (Colossians 2:6-7; Galatians 5:16, 25), trusting God's wisdom in His Word and empowerment through His Spirit to shape a life that is pleasing to Him. Concluding with the phrase "with fear and trembling," Paul added a sobering reminder of a believer's accountability to God that is demonstrated through God's temporal discipline and ultimate judgment before Christ. For the believer, the issue is not losing a relationship with God but squandering the privilege of partnership with Him in ways that impact this life and eternity.

Although our faithfulness to work out our salvation often falters, God's faithfulness in accomplishing His purpose remains consistent, certain, and perfect (John 5:17). The question is never whether God will fulfill His purpose through His creation, but if we will respond in obedience (Job 42:2; Psalm 33:11; Proverbs 16:4, 19:21; Isaiah 46:10-11; Acts 17:26). Daily opportunities exist for each believer to be engaged in fruitful ministry, but this blessing can be missed through disobedience, distraction, or ignorance. Paul assured his readers that God's purpose will be realized through His power (Ephesians 1:19, 5:18; Philippians 2:13), ultimately in harmony with His pleasure (Ephesians 1:5, 9). As "cracked pots" empowered by God, we are incapable of fully grasping either of these realities, but the key to our engagement with God involves faithful obedience, not a comprehensive understanding of how God works (2 Corinthians 4:7-12).

Paul emphasized our obedient partnership with Him, calling believers to live above reproach as those who "shine as lights" (Philippians 2:15; Matthew 5:16) in a dark world that is hostile toward God. He commanded his readers to cease grumbling and avoid the angry disputes that such behavior provoked. Obedience to Paul's exhortation is foundational for promoting peace and love among believers and stimulating the interest of people who have not yet trusted Christ. As Jesus told His disciples, people will know we are Christians by our love (John 13:35). Mutual encouragement with believers and meaningful friendships with those who do not yet know Jesus provide opportunities for fruitful obedience to this exhortation.

Relationships with Believers

Following the pattern in this passage, relationships among believers invite initial consideration. Specific admonitions undergird the relationships that help God's people shine brightly in a world of grumbling and fear. Key aspects of healthy relationships amid such a difficult environment include *proactive forgiveness* when offended by others, *persistent love* as we bless others, and *prompt reconciliation* when we harm others.

In a world where hurt remains rampant and anger inevitable, learning to address anger through *proactive forgiveness* becomes critical. Paul assumed the Ephesian believers would experience anger, yet showed them how to address their anger without being derailed spiritually (Ephesians 4:15, 26-27, 32). Many reasons exist for relational conflicts, which provoke anger—people are different, communication is challenging, change is stressful and sinful wounds are common. But keep in mind, if anger is allowed to linger and spawn bitterness, relationships are damaged and spiritual fruitfulness is compromised (Ephesians 4:29-30).

Anger, like love, is expressed in different ways. Three common anger "languages" are explosion, suppression, and passive aggression. Most people have a dominant tendency but are capable of multiple destructive patterns. Explosion helps the exploder feel relief momentarily while others grapple with the trauma of the moment. Suppressors feel they are controlling the anger and may even see it as a spiritual virtue; however, suppressed anger becomes increasingly obvious to others and eventually poisons the suppressor. It will lead to an unexplainable explosion or depression for those most capable of suppression. Passive-aggressive people sabotage relationships while cheerfully denying their anger. When confronted, they are masters at denial and avoidance. The devastating consequences of this approach can destroy marriages, families, churches, and teams in a variety of contexts, all while denying any problems.

Unresolved anger hurts people and damages relationships. Two common responses that compound these relational consequences are avoiding the issue (the "flight" response) and attacking the person (the "fight" response). Paul challenged believers to reject both and address personal anger issues honestly (Ephesians 4:15), promptly (Ephesians 4:26–27), and privately (Ephesians 4:15; Matthew 5:23–25), forgiving those who hurt them because God has forgiven believers in Christ (Ephesians 4:32). Forgiveness is costly. It often requires absorbing the hurt and pain of another person's sin to release the person from relational debt. There is always a cost and sometimes a substantial one. But continued bitterness toward a person becomes emotionally corrosive and spiritually destructive—an even greater consequence.

Forgiveness is critical to our spiritual and emotional health and essential for healthy relationships. *It is more like a path than an event,* affirming a posture of unconditional forgiveness is required as our experiences and memories are unpacked. As we grow toward Christ-centered maturity and consistently forgive others because Christ forgave us, we experience freedom and fruitfulness. It also is helpful to remember that Christ paid for the sins of those who hurt us. God has planned and provided for forgiveness; He is our model for forgiveness that addresses life's hurts while making restored relationships possible. Helping family and friends learn how to follow this pattern will release a multitude of blessings as an essential element of preparing fruitful multipliers.[1]

As we proactively forgive others, believers are called to *persistently love each other*. Over fifty "one another" commands are found in the Scriptures and reveal the urgency for helping each other toward maturity.[2] Obedience to these specific exhortations contributes to relationships among believers who honor God and seek to bless people regardless of their response to God (Romans 12:17-21). The core command, love one another, is repeated fifteen times (John 13:34-35, 15:12, 17; Romans 12:1, 13:8; 1 Thessalonians 4:9; 1 Peter 3:8; 1 John 3:11, 23, 4:7, 11, 12; 2 John 5).

The remaining commands include: encourage one another (1 Thessalonians 4:18, 5:11; Hebrews 3:13, 10:25), forgive one another (Ephesians 4:32; Colossians 3:13), teach one another (Romans 15:14; Colossians 3:16), and admonish one another (Romans 15:14), all done with humility and compassion (Ephesians 4:32; Colossians 3:16; Philippians 2:3; 1 Peter 5:5). Expressions of tender love are helpful in our relationships; however, there are times when tough love that confronts the destructiveness of sin directly is needed. Enabling behaviors that damage people and relationships is not loving (Matthew 18:15-17). The wisdom for this balance of tender and tough love can only be given by God who promises this blessing for those living in humble dependence (James 1:5–7). Tough love requires an extra measure of compassion, reflecting sadness rather than anger at the situation or person. Gaining skills in this aspect of faithful ministry becomes a critical issue for multipliers. When believers love one another, churches experience peace and unity, strengthening all involved. It also is evidence of our relationship with Christ and a powerful part of God working to draw people to His Son (John 6:44, 13:35).

A third biblical exhortation that strengthens relationships and broadens ministry opportunities involves *pursuing reconciliation with people we have harmed.* If unresolved, this issue has a substantial negative impact on our worship (Matthew 5:23-24). When we find ourselves in situations where we have offended others, God's Spirit is faithful to show us our sins and guide us to promptly confess our sins to God. As God's Word promises, this agreement with God enables us to experience the cleansing and forgiveness of sin, restoring fellowship with God (1 John 1:9).

This blessing does not remove the temporal consequences of sin. But it does provide an opportunity for a new beginning in the relationship. As we obey Jesus's instruction to pursue reconciliation with those we have hurt, we do so as humble, forgiven people. Confident that God's amazing grace can prepare significant opportunities when we acknowledge our sin, believers should ask the offended person for forgiveness and seek relational healing. The surprise and even suspicion of someone who has been hurt may be overcome by Spirit-empowered honesty and humility that leads to reconciliation.

It is always possible that the person will rebuff a restored relationship since both parties must embrace this blessing. Continuing in prayer for the person offended and looking for ways to bless him or her would be a wise response, demonstrating humility before God, commitment to healthy relationships, and confidence that God's grace is greater than our sin both in forgiveness before Him and in life's relationships.

Relating to People Who Need Jesus

As people obey Christ by addressing anger, blessing relationships, and pursuing reconciliation, they are positioned for a privilege that is only enjoyed in this life—sharing the message of salvation that is found in Jesus Christ. God gives a gift of evangelism to some spiritual leaders[3] to fulfill His purpose of equipping everyone for this ministry of explaining their hope in Christ to those who have questions (Acts 1:8; 2 Corinthians 5:20-21; Colossians4:5-6; 1 Peter 3:15). A perspective that helps believers experience this privilege prioritizes a unique sphere of influence for each person. Your family, neighbors, coworkers, parents of your children's friends, acquaintances at the gym, friends in a community service club, and anyone else around you enough to "smell" the aroma of Christ are part of a dynamic network.

Each believer lives on the "front lines" for evangelism. In spontaneous events, a person may join the sphere for just a few pivotal moments as God works in circumstances that He prepares. While inviting friends to a church event can be positive, inviting a neighbor to a ballgame may offer a more fruitful opportunity for spiritual influence. Seeing life through this relational prism helps maximize the blessing of lifestyle evangelism in a matrix of relational connections through which God can draw people to Christ.

Relational Credibility

God is working to expand a person's spiritual influence. A catalyst for such a meaningful impact for Christ is *living with authentic credibility*. When I arrived in Eastern Turkey in January 1975 as an Air Force officer, I desired to see how God would work during a year spent monitoring the Soviet missile program. It was soon clear that Major Adams was the most credible person on our small, remote base. When I asked his counsel on how to maximize the year spiritually, he gave two exhortations without hesitation: "If you are not going to do your job well, forcing others to work harder because of your negligence, please do not tell anyone you are a Christian. And if you are not going to live like an authentic believer, on and off the job, seek God's forgiveness and help before you start talking about Jesus." His exhortation revealed a high value on credibility.

This paradigm helps clarify the central elements of credibility.[4]

Character + Competence + Consistency = Credibility

Character means a person exhibits the qualities that inspire trust in a relationship. Paul's list of qualifications for elders in a church provides a portrait of the person with credibility (1 Timothy 3:1–13; Titus 1:5–9). *Competence* signifies the skills and discipline required to make an excellent contribution in your vocation and relationships. If your engagement in life's responsibilities helps others be more effective, you are also demonstrating competence. *Consistency* means you have modeled character and competence long enough that people perceive you as a trusted source of wisdom in a career, ministry, or relationship. In summary, *credibility* means people will listen with respect when you speak. Personal credibility joined with biblical preparation strengthens a clear presentation of the Gospel to others.

Amid life's painful experiences, people often follow Job, David, and Habakkuk by asking, "Why?" God embraces us in those moments while rarely giving us an answer (Psalm 34:18). But part of the answer to "what" God is doing in our worst experiences is related to credibility. We never look or pray for hardship because it will find us soon enough. But in those seasons, *believers who draw near to God and continue with character, competence, and consistency as He sustains them on the path of suffering, grieving, and healing can discover even greater credibility.* God wastes none of our pain and works to enlarge our privilege of being His instrument. People with great credibility usually have influence amplified by spiritual or circumstantial suffering (1 Peter 4:12-19).

Specific, Personal Prayer

With credibility as a foundation, the enduring catalyst for fruitful evangelism is persistent prayer. Paul modeled this pattern while imprisoned in Rome for his faithfulness to Christ. His new sphere of influence centered on the rotating guards assigned to his house arrest. Paul noted some of them had become believers (Philippians 1:13). He was praying for specific people already in his life. The more we pray for individuals we know, the more God opens opportunities with them and people we encounter spontaneously. As he concluded his letter to the Colossian church, Paul exhorted fellow believers to be devoted to prayer—literally "stick to prayer" (Colossians 4:2-4). This exhortation is a thread throughout his letters (Romans 12:11–12; Ephesians 6:18; 1 Thessalonians 5:17), which often includes lengthy prayers.

When I consider consistency in prayer, I am sometimes discouraged by how easily I am distracted. In 1968, the industrial giant

Minnesota Mining and Manufacturing Company (3M) explored new, stronger adhesives for its products. One of its experimental adhesives demonstrated insufficient strength for their purposes. In 1973, new corporate leadership brought a perspective valuing this limited adhesive. It led to the Post-it Notes now found all around the world.[5] Whether a person's "stickiness" is permanent glue or Post-it Note strength, keep praying with the confidence that the Spirit helps us even in our weakness (Romans 8:26-27).[6]

As believers pray, they must remain alert to what God is doing, especially during painful circumstances (Ephesians 6:18; Colossians 4:2). This perspective is possible through persistent gratitude for all God has done for us. Though imprisoned unjustly, Paul's enthusiasm for how God was working had been strengthened by truths outlined in an earlier letter to the Corinthians.[7] When Paul looked back, he saw God's merciful salvation in Christ. When he examined the multiple distresses of the present, he saw God's power revealed through his frailty. When he looked to the future, he saw the glory of God, which makes all distress in life appear momentary and light. It is always too soon to lose heart. Unshakable hope in life's hardest moments communicates a magnetic message, surprising people who live in a sea of grumbling complaints.

The priority of our grateful prayers is not relief from our current circumstances, but faithfulness to God in our sphere of relational influence. Paul understood every person, even a member of the elite Praetorian guard, needed the salvation only Jesus could provide; therefore, he perceived his current relational context as rich with spiritual opportunity. Paul urged his readers to pray with him for open doors to communicate the amazing message of salvation through faith in Christ. In a letter to the Ephesians, written during that same imprisonment, Paul added the dimension of fearlessness in prayer (Ephesians 6:18). With a grateful heart and a fearless spirit (2 Timothy 1:7), Paul requested prayer for the biblical message about humanity's sin and God's loving provision in Christ to be presented with clarity.

As believers pray with gratitude and endurance, Paul exhorted them to persuade others through engaging, gracious conversations that reflected authentic intimacy with God (Colossians 4:5–6). A transformed life marked by integrity, compassion, and joy strengthens relationships while provoking curiosity and stimulating questions. Such intimacy with God inevitably results in a person having an aroma of Christ (2 Corinthians 2:14–16). How people respond to His aroma will vary and is not the issue determining the faithfulness of a witness.

Building Fruitful Bridges

An intentional focus on building bridges with others who do not yet know Christ enlarges our sphere of influence. God uses people in evangelistic conversations who have discovered ways to build friendships outside of the Christian cocoon. Family, neighbors, coworkers, fellow parents, and acquaintances can become friends open to spiritual conversations. As mutual interests are developed, possibilities for positive shared experiences multiply. Being a caring neighbor, including a family in community events, or sharing a cup of coffee with a friend before work can be as significant as being imprisoned with an elite guard in ancient Rome.

Like Jesus, who received criticism for spending too much time with tax collectors and sinners (Mark 2:15-17), we should not expect people to behave like believers before trusting Christ. How new friends talk and what they value is not the issue. The integrity of a believer's life can be valued without policing the life of a person who needs a Savior. As these relationships grow, opportunities to express compassion and celebration will unfold.

Gracious responses to these circumstances reveal that the most hardened skeptic often responds to kindness in hard times and celebration in happy times, if offered with no strings attached.

As believers live with the joy only found in Christ, they can include others in their activities and engage with new friends.

Genuine interest in others expressed in honest questions may lead to spiritual conversations. Both Paul and Peter emphasized questions by interested people in their exhortations regarding evangelism (Colossians 4:5–6; 1 Peter 3:14-16). One of the ways to encourage questions is to ask questions that reflect genuine concern for others. Believers should not be surprised by occasional hostility in these conversations (2 Corinthians 2:16, 4:7-12; 1 Peter 2:12, 3:14-16). Hostility toward Christ must not be inflamed by angry reactions by believers. As a forgiving posture and enduring concern for the person is maintained, God may enrich future conversations with greater openness to spiritual truth.

While developing friendships with people who do not yet know Christ, believers are called to make the most of every opportunity to explain the gospel (Ephesians 5:15-16). As they continue to depend on God's empowerment, they should expect spiritual conversations with friends as well as spontaneous encounters. The preparation required for gentle and respectful answers (1 Peter 3:15) becomes a core element of the wisdom needed for interaction with those who are not followers of Christ. Every step toward maturity in Christ amplifies this preparation. But Peter specifically mentioned the need to give answers for the hope that believers have in Christ. Careful study and discerning skills in both asking questions and giving answers are essential for a person to be equipped for fruitful evangelistic conversations.

God's wisdom is required to make spiritual conversations personal and practical. The benefit of writing the message out in simple pictures on a napkin or piece of paper includes both clarity in the conversation and an opportunity to give a written review of the message with contact information for future conversations.[8] A prepared person also needs a biblical perspective. As believers engage in evangelistic conversations, they are joining God as He draws people toward Jesus (John 5:17, 6:44). This perspective encourages believers to share the Gospel calmly and clearly as God's messengers, confident the response of their friend is ultimately between him or her and God. It also strengthens the emphasis on gracious communication (Colossians 4:6), stimulating engagement through good questions, honest answers, and personal interest. This perspective shapes the gentleness and respect that is essential for meaningful spiritual conversations. It also stimulates the urgent desire for others to receive the gift of salvation found only in Christ while encouraging ongoing friendships. These earthly conversations are experienced with anticipation of the celebration that erupts in heaven every time a sinner responds to God's grace (Luke 15:10).

The blessing of spiritual intimacy with God and significant partnership in God's redemptive purpose is an awesome privilege. This unfolds day by day, each with lasting significance. Embracing this privilege includes encouraging growing believers toward maturity and preparing fruitful multipliers as we engage people who are not yet believers. This pattern also provides a delightful bonus—personal refreshment and theological perspective that enriches every opportunity for ministry.

An Encouraging Thread

Almost 800 years after Patrick's influential ministry, moral and spiritual corruption flourished in the Medieval Church. Accumulating massive wealth, exercising control over uneducated masses, launching crusades against Muslims, and battling uncooperative kings created a spiritual vacuum among the millions attending services in a language they did not understand. God continued working, preparing new wineskins for the spiritual refreshment that resulted from a clear message of personal salvation in Christ.

Although many factors contributed to the Reformation centuries later, two are critical to an emphasis on discipleship. First, the Bible was translated into languages understood by the people. Peter Waldo (1140-1218) from Lyon, France decided to follow Christ in a life of poverty and preaching. After translating portions of Scripture into French, Waldo and his followers began preaching without church approval, quickly drawing the ire of the archbishop who controlled preaching in his bishopric.[9] The rejection of church authority and a careful study of Scripture led his excommunicated followers to denounce purgatory and to embrace prayers for the dead and the mediation of priests and transubstantiation. This led to persecution and rapid expansion even after Waldo's leadership ended.[10]

Almost two centuries later, a leading theology professor at Oxford named John Wycliffe (d. 1384) became another pivotal contributor to spiritual renewal. He initially challenged the Roman Church regarding the authority of political leaders to seize the property of corrupt clergy.[11] Wycliffe's criticisms intensified as the papacy spiraled into the chaos of the Great Schism with multiple popes each claiming authority.[12] When he declared the Pope was the Antichrist, the papacy was poisonous, and Christ alone was the head of the church, only a large group of supporters prevented a harsh response. When the Old and New Testaments were translated into English under Wycliffe's leadership, a host of preachers began teaching God's Word. When the people evaluated the teaching and practices of the priests by the standard of Scripture, the impetus for dramatic change gained momentum.

Second, the truths of Scripture (Romans 12:1-8; Ephesians 4:7-16; 1 Peter 4:10) amplified an emphasis on the priesthood of all believers. Waldo and Wycliffe modeled and taught this truth. John Huss, a priest in Prague influenced by Wycliffe's writings in the fifteenth century, began to oppose abuses by clergy and veneration of the Pope. He taught only Christ can forgive sins and all believers can know and serve God without priestly mediation. Though burned at the stake in 1415 for his views,[13] Huss's teachings spread throughout his followers.[14] The opportunity to learn the truths of Scripture in their own language and experience the blessings of personal intimacy with God began to penetrate the Roman Catholic Church in ways that prompted profound changes in the sixteenth century.

The Reformation, led by Luther, Calvin, Zwingli, and others, challenged the dominance of the Roman Catholic Church, especially regarding issues related to personal salvation. These men, and those they influenced, presented views eventually summarized as the Five Solas: We are saved in Christ alone, by grace alone, through faith alone, with the Scriptures alone being the only infallible rule of faith and practice, and for the glory of God alone.[15]

Most of the Reformation churches remained linked to local or national governments,[16] hindering the spontaneous expansion of the church, a distinguishing characteristic of the early church.[17] Disputes over views of the Lord's Supper,[18] executions for adult baptisms,[19] and aggressive reaction from the Roman Catholic Church contributed to tumult within and among European nations[20] in the late sixteenth and much of the seventeenth centuries. This political consequence with tragic human costs reflected competing religious systems that were fighting for control. Such turmoil delayed a vigorous emphasis on sharing the Gospel message as well as the affirmation of intimacy with God and ministry for all believers. The impact of this transformative thread in widespread mission endeavors remained centuries in the future. God's transforming grace affirmed among people in Europe would eventually be proclaimed globally through faithful people.

9

ENLARGING THE JOY OF MULTIPLICATION

Having explained a clear and challenging pattern for intentional, strategic multiplication, Paul commanded Timothy to reflect on the exhortation he had just received, allowing the Lord to show him the specifics of what faithfulness to this privilege meant as a dedicated soldier, disciplined athlete, and diligent farmer (2 Timothy 2). While relating to all followers of Christ, this perspective encourages multipliers to focus on believers who are eager to learn more about serving God by blessing others. This opportunity can be pursued with the confidence that *Jesus still selects multipliers, and prepared multipliers can identify and invest in those Jesus is inviting.*

A Persistent Emphasis on Identifying Multipliers

From Jesus's example with His apostles and Paul's exhortation to Timothy, the faithful comprise only a portion of the multitude. The presence of maturing multipliers, committed to humble dependence on God and looking for ways to engage in whatever God has prepared for them, will encourage large and small gatherings of believers. Seeking to be faithful to the multitudes while staying focused on preparing multipliers requires a persistent emphasis on identifying and engaging fruitful people.

As people begin a relationship with Jesus, they join with the large number of believers who are privileged to pursue maturity with the possibility of preparation as multipliers. Encouraging new believers in the initial patterns of spiritual growth offers an opportunity to gauge the faithfulness of someone who may be a multiplier. As they continue to discover the joy of serving God, discussing ways to help others experience this blessing would be expected.

Jesus's twelve disciples were not necessarily mature, but they were faithful.[1] A faithful young believer often possesses more potential as a fruitful multiplier than a distracted, discouraged long-term follower of Christ.

Conversations and ministry experiences with growing Christians present natural opportunities to discover those who are open to investing in other faithful people. A contagious, joyful, credible believer becomes a person others will follow and trust. To discover an appropriate time to initiate this intentional process, a prepared multiplier must confirm the maturing believer is faithful, available, intentional, teachable, and possesses a heart for God's strategy of spiritual multiplication.[2] First, those who are *faithful* are reliable, with the integrity and consistency essential for fruitful ministry. Second, an *available person* will invest the time necessary to become a well-prepared multiplier. Many faithful people are presently in circumstances that keep them from pursuing such a ministry. Third, a person must be *intentional*, understanding the value of investing in people who will be able to identify and equip others. Fourth, believers must be *teachable*, willing to learn from the person who equips them initially, and to continue learning from each person they prepare as a multiplier. Finally, a spiritual reproducer must have a *heart for God's strategy for spiritual multiplication,* seen as a privilege with earthly and heavenly blessings.

The process of identifying faithful multipliers often originates in casual conversations. A simple, "How are things going?" can be dismissed by "Fine." It can also be an opportunity to tell a Christian friend how God is encouraging you through intentional discipleship. If there is curiosity, a brief visit will allow you to gauge interest in this rewarding experience. Another starting point involves asking your friend how he or she is doing spiritually. This interaction usually provides an opportunity for spiritual encouragement, but you must be prepared for a friend to ask about your relationship with Christ. If this happens, explaining the blessing of intentional discipleship would be appropriate. If the person does not inquire about your life, it may be an indicator the friend does not presently have the concern for others that is essential as a multiplier.

Strategic multipliers value a preemptive commitment to a pattern of intentional investment with other faithful believers. When believers know they will be discussing these truths with another faithful person in a few months, they prepare differently, ask questions more carefully, take notes more diligently (many even record the conversations to use when they are preparing to lead the conversations themselves), and begin praying for their first faithful person from the initial conversation. This launch point also addresses the issue of when to end regular meetings. Both will become partners in multiplication with others while meeting occasionally for support and encouragement.

Once it becomes clear a person possesses the qualities essential for fruitful ministry, there must be clarity about the challenge of both the preparation and the enduring privilege of equipping other multipliers. Giving a person time to pray, discuss with a spouse and friends, and soberly discern God's direction in life is essential for a strong start in this growth experience. It is important for a person to begin in willing obedience to God, not under pressure to please someone else.

My brother, Ron, described this as "giving people an off-ramp," continuing an encouraging relationship even if a person is unavailable for this opportunity. If a person decides to begin an intentional discipleship process, you must place appropriate responsibility on the partner to prepare for each conversation as well as sustain communication about the meetings. If the lead partner is working harder than the person being equipped, it is a warning signal that the process may yield more struggle than spiritual progress. Since timing is important, this is another place where an off-ramp, joined with a less challenging relational engagement, might be a wise step to take.

If people want to learn about the concepts in the *Launching Multipliers!* resource but do not desire to prepare as a multiplier, we encourage them to download the resource and work through the sessions by themselves or with a friend. In some instances, it may be possible to work through two or three key conversations with them to provide exposure to the methodological distinctions if they intend to use the resource with others (see Appendix).

If this period of clarification and honest communication leads to a commitment to prepare as an intentional multiplier, weekly discussions begin when the partner has completed the preparation of the initial session. The conversations in the process are designed to equip a person for an eternally significant mission, not just to complete a spiritual program.

Each session presents opportunities for specific steps of obedience to Christ. With mutual encouragement, both partners experience the transformation that affirms the credibility God uses to enlarge spiritual influence. The initial session explains a simple, clear presentation of the Gospel, equipping the partner to have ongoing, honest conversations with friends who have spiritual questions. This privilege is strengthened step by step and is consistent with the evangelistic urgency found in Christ's mandate to make disciples.

A Distinctive Focus for Intentional Multiplication

In Paul's letter to Titus, he emphasized how investing in others shapes the practice of men working with men and women with women (Titus 2:1–8). These conversations inevitably become quite intimate as believers share their hearts and struggles in many areas of life: personal, marriage, parenting, and career relationships. A mature believer usually outside of your family (and sometimes outside of your career setting) will have perspectives that invigorate honest discussions, especially about areas where you have struggles. The model given to Titus addresses foundational spiritual nurturing where part of the discussion addresses the challenges of being a godly man or woman. The wisdom of men with men and women with women increases the likely benefits and diminishes possible challenges during the spiritual transparency of this process.[3]

With a Few Surprises

One of the surprises I have experienced during years of intentional preparation of multipliers indicates how a relatively young believer who understands the methodology of the conversations can be an effective lead partner with a more mature believer. The younger believer (in terms of years following Christ) helps the more mature partner discover skills and methods that enrich structured and spontaneous conversations. The more mature partner usually shares insights and asks questions that stimulate the biblical and theological progress of the younger partner. Both are reminded in each session that following Jesus and maintaining genuine humility before Him is foundational.

Several years ago, I knew a businessman with a technical background who became equipped as a multiplier and discipled several men in his church. When he had the opportunity to work with a seminary student from India who was pursuing a PhD in theology, he hesitated. He correctly perceived the student already knew more theology than he might ever grasp. Encouraged to go forward in faith and humility, the result became powerful for both. The student had little knowledge about conversations that use questions to discover biblical, theological, and spiritual insights.

The relational and ministry growth of the student matched the theological insights of the tech-oriented businessman. The student returned to India for a teaching opportunity that involved what he had learned through his conversations with the businessman. Another man equipped his father, his most influential mentor, to launch multipliers. Since the conversations are designed to allow both partners to share insights and ask questions with a persistent value on humility, *it is not a teacher/student experience but one in which both partners encourage the other person as Christ's disciple.*

Another surprise pertains to the ways people have used our conversations in new settings. One of the people discipled at a church in Fort Worth moved to northern Virginia for a new job. He shared a copy of our eighteen sessions with a friend at an area church.

Though he decided to attend another church and did not discuss the materials with his associate, people in Northern Virginia began to download the *Launching Multipliers!* resource. We asked this partner if he knew about it. After a brief inquiry, he discovered his friend had shared the resource with others at church and their men's ministry adapted our strategy. They cover the first six sessions in small groups with lots of paired discussions. Those who complete the initial sessions have an opportunity to pursue the remaining conversations in a one-on-one setting. We are delighted to discover new ways that creative people use biblical resources in diverse circumstances.

When people inquire about our current ministry, I often tell them our goal is to help growing Christians enjoy their daily involvement in God's purposes so authentically that others will be curious. Believers will want to discover what is happening in their lives and people who do not yet trust Christ will have honest questions. Intentional, strategic multiplication prepares a person for this kind of privilege as a delightful "first fruit" of God's rewards.

Preparing Multipliers, Not Finishing a Program

Having laid out a clear and challenging pattern for intentional, strategic, relational multiplication, Paul commanded Timothy to reflect on the exhortation he had just received (2 Timothy 2:1-7). While pondering this demanding but rewarding opportunity, this privilege must be examined considering the blessings received in Christ. Allow the Lord to show the person specifics of what this privilege will mean for a faithful believer. Consistent obedience to biblical commands and principles is joined with a persistent emphasis on spiritual multiplication. When a believer knows he or she will be leading discussions in a few months, their eagerness to explore the questions and grasp the answers is stimulated each week. Within weeks, prayer for faithful people leads to conversations about ways to discern a person's willingness to embrace the challenges of preparing as a multiplier. While many prefer to complete the process before starting with their first partner, some are ready to begin sooner. Flexibility about the pace of your discussions (weekly or meeting twice a month) values the progress and growth of the maturing partner who is ready to begin with another faithful person.

In some situations, it becomes clear a believer is not ready to pursue an intensive season of spiritual preparation. It may be a lack of genuine interest or practical availability. In either case, help the person take an "off-ramp" while affirming your desire to continue an encouraging relationship in a less structured way. Offering to read a book of their choice and discuss it over coffee might be a way to move forward while making long-term relational investments with committed multipliers. This approach helps a fruitful multiplier make the most of opportunities to encourage others while equipping a few fruitful individuals in ways that transform life and touch eternity.

When people know they will be discussing these concepts with another faithful person in a few months, they study differently, ask questions more carefully, take notes more diligently (many even record the conversations for use when they lead the conversations themselves), and begin praying for their first faithful person in the initial conversation. These biblical truths must be absorbed in a context that encourages transparency, strengthens accountability, and nurtures God-honoring motivations. After months of meeting weekly, discussing the truths, developing the skills, and cultivating the attitudes pursued in these sessions, a deep friendship and spiritual partnership will emerge.

While equipping a multiplier, there is flexibility to discuss issues like marriage, parenting, work challenges, ministry issues, and personal struggles. Each conversation contains a clear path for which both people have prepared. During an opportunity for prayer requests, pressing concerns may refocus aspects of the conversation. The discussions also encourage participants to ask questions about biblical passages and theological issues as well as personal concerns that affect their ability to be useful to God.

Conversations with pastors, missionaries, and seminary students often include mentoring and coaching conversations that address not only their biblical concerns but also their distinctive gifts, opportunities, environments, and challenges. For business leaders, many aspects of their jobs involve relational matters and integrity issues. Wisely addressing such concerns will amplify their spiritual influence. Unlike an urgent personal issue, such discussions may be pursued in an additional conversation for a specific purpose. But the lead partner assumes responsibility for pacing the discussions so that such learning opportunities are not neglected, because *the goal is preparing a fruitful person, not finishing a program.*

A clear launch point addresses an issue that may challenge some discipleship relationships. The transition to an encouraging friendship without first spending consistent time together may be difficult. Since partners are told at the beginning of the process about investing in others, praying for and identifying a first multiplier becomes a part of the entire experience. Coaching the partner through this critical step and helping them begin to meet with their first partner, sometimes even before completion of the initial eighteen conversations, becomes one of the most helpful ways to encourage a healthy "launch."

After discussing the final session, take a week to review the entire experience, celebrate how God is working toward multiplication opportunities, and commit your friend and partner to friendship in the season ahead. Since a prepared partner will start meeting with someone else regularly, it is a reality to be faced. Both will become partners in multiplication who get together occasionally for support and encouragement, celebrating what God is doing through new friendships. Since God delights in selfless humility, these transitions reflect the values of intentional preparation of multipliers.

While ongoing, regular meetings are unlikely with each multiplier, mutual encouragement in groups of multipliers can be a blessing. Like Jesus and Paul, committed spiritual multipliers today must continue to invest in those they launch. Giving a prepared multiplier a copy of an overview of theology can encourage fruitful living and ministry while helping answer specific questions prompted by discipleship discussions.[4] Reading and discussing other books with a group of multipliers help sharpen their understanding of biblical issues and cultivate relationships with other fruitful people.

These ongoing relationships require a pattern of personal encouragement in the context of *constrained availability*. Moses sent Joshua into battle while remaining in prayer on the mountain (Exodus 17:8-17), and Jesus sent His disciples throughout Israel as lambs among wolves to proclaim the kingdom of God, encouraging their full reliance on His provision (Luke 9:1-11, 10:1-24). Paul deployed Timothy, Titus, and others for leadership in churches to give them room to discover God's faithfulness without their mentor. This pattern becomes a critical step in the growth that God guides. This relational distance affirms what has been emphasized throughout months of intentional conversations: every partner is a disciple of Jesus directly. In my case, none of the scores of men I have equipped are *my* disciples. They are now partners in preparing other disciples of Jesus as multipliers.

Several ways exist to leverage a normal pattern of personal ministry to nurture those being discipled, as well as those who have completed preparation as a multiplier. As partners serve in various ministry settings, they continue modeling the servanthood that is discussed and demonstrated during one-on-one meetings.

Jesus's pattern as He trained His disciples leveraged shared ministry experiences. Including a partner as a leader for a discipleship retreat or mobilizing a small group of multipliers to encourage another church or ministry can be particularly joyful. Shared ministry in a local church or a missions endeavor offers enriching encouragement for partners in multiplication. At the heart of this strategy is the conviction to live in community with other believers. Such a community becomes healthier as people live and share the truths learned in discipleship conversations.

After years of launching multipliers, my circle of trusted friends increasingly includes people who are now partners in spiritual multiplication. Some have launched many others and stimulated discipleship ministries focused on equipping spiritual leaders in the United States and other nations. Others have invested in faithful people while steadily serving as pastors, elders, and fruitful servants in local churches. A delightful outcome involves witnessing how God accomplishes more than I could have imagined through these faithful friends. It illustrates the "first fruits" for diligent servants in God's harvest.

For pastors, and others involved in vocational ministry, the refreshment experienced when faithful people discover the joy of serving God delivers a powerful blessing. Pastoral burnout is an epidemic because ministry is difficult and has been since apostolic times.[5] Losing heart is a chronic issue (Hebrews 12:1-3). A surprise benefit of one-on-one discipleship is the refreshment found in the theological perspective (2 Corinthians 4:1-18) and relational connection (1 Thessalonians 2:1-20) experienced in each conversation. *A few hours of preparing multipliers each week will strengthen refreshment, endurance, and hope for faithful leaders.*

An Encouraging Thread

During the late seventeenth century, some of the best elements of Reformation teaching began to take root alongside and beyond the state-connected churches. The grace of God prevailed in many settings as people studied Scripture in their own language and learned to serve God in their lives. The priesthood of all believers became a defining emphasis for a network of leaders who had a heart for intimacy with God, a commitment to unity among believers, and a passion for evangelism and missions.

A pastor and theologian named Philip Jacob Spener in Frankfurt, a Hebrew professor named August Hermann Francke in Halle, and a nobleman named Nikolaus Ludwig von Zinzendorf in Herrnhut became key German contributors to a movement known as Pietism. Zinzendorf, who studied under Franke and associated with the Hussite group known as the Bohemian Brethren,[6] provided his estate for the group called Moravians. The pietistic view of spirituality emphasized a personal relationship with God, bearing the practical fruit of faith. Evangelism, and missions in harmony with these values, flourished through the theological preaching and writing of faithful men like George Whitefield and Jonathan Edwards, leading to revival movements impacting the spiritual climate in America and England.

Among the multiple blessings of these revival meetings, there was an urgency about global missions experienced in a wide range of evangelical churches. William Carey (1761- 1834) studied Latin and Greek and explored world geography while he repaired shoes in England. He became an independent Baptist pastor who taught that the Great Commission still applied to believers and repeated a mantra, "Expect great things for God; attempt great things for God."[7] He demonstrated these values when he relocated his family to India, studied the languages intently, and, eventually, gathered a team to translate the entire Bible into six languages (with portions in many others). He started schools and colleges, promoted agricultural improvements, fought for the protection of widows, and encouraged Indian believers in lifestyle evangelism.[8]

Carey never left India; however, his book, *An Enquiry into the Obligation of Christians to Use Means for the Conversion of the Heathens* (1792), and years of communication with the Baptist Missionary Society that he helped start, ignited an awareness of global missions far beyond his circle of supporters. Carey became known as the "Father of Modern Missions."[9] His exhortation and example prompted hundreds of faithful people drawn to Christ through the evangelical revivals in England and America in the eighteenth century to invest their lives as missionaries, primarily in Asia and Africa.[10]

This passion for global missions continues into the present. Whether in independent organizations or denominational agencies, these ministries generally emphasize core elements of Reformation teaching and follow methods with pietistic roots. Whether in local or global settings, helping people begin a relationship with Christ and make incremental progress toward spiritual maturity are core aspects of equipping leaders who could expand their strategy globally.

Groups that sought to provide benevolence to hurting people, like the YMCA (1846) and the Salvation Army (1865), originally emphasized discipleship. Ministries with students like InterVarsity (1877), the Navigators (1933), Young Life (1941), Cru (1951) as well as numerous camping ministries have made discipleship a core emphasis. Mission agencies like China Inland Mission (1861) and Greater Europe Mission (1949) represent hundreds of evangelistic and church-planting missions among the nations that are fueled by a legacy of discipleship efforts, which are centuries in the making. It is amazing to ponder in the present, but the beauty and joy of each thread in the tapestry of God's grace of multiplication in Jesus Christ will never be exhausted in eternity. God's glory, revealed through His gracious work in Jesus, will prompt spontaneous joy in Christ beyond our wildest imagination (Ephesians 3:20-21).

ANTICIPATING ETERNAL REWARDS

Paul described such blessings in ministry in this life, often in hard situations, as "first fruits," a fulfilling appetizer of the joys of heaven. (1 Timothy 6:17-19; 2 Timothy 2:6). Faithful ministry rooted in humility before God and motivated by gratitude for Christ leads to daily opportunities that are marked by thanksgiving and hope. Amid great adversity (2 Corinthians 4:7-12) Paul urged thanksgiving to the God who always leads us in His triumph (2 Corinthians 2:14-16) with spiritual blessings, motivating faithfulness to God that results in eternal rewards.

A seminary student recently mentioned several friends who refused to discuss the issue of eternal rewards. Their concern was that emphasizing rewards could stimulate comparison, prompting discouragement or arrogance. This comment reflects other conversations I have experienced during decades of ministry. How can we anticipate rewards in heaven without being distracted in relationships and ministry now?

The more critical question is why Jesus, Paul, and others would urge believers to lay up treasure in heaven (Matthew 6:19–21; 1 Timothy 6:17-19). This chapter unpacks biblical teaching on eternal rewards as motivation for faithful earthly ministry and stimulation for glorious eternal worship.

Individual Judgment is God's Plan

One of the dominant threads in God's Word maintains that people are created as stewards of God (Genesis 2:15-17; 1 Corinthians 4:2; Philippians 2:9-11), and all individuals will give an account of their lives to God (Matthew 12:36; Romans 14:12; 1 Corinthians 3:5-4:7; 2 Corinthians 5:9-10; Revelation 20:11-15); however, our focus pertains to the judgment of believers in Christ at the Bema Seat when every believer will stand before God. This *certainty* is expressed in biblical declarations, stating wisdom begins with the fear of the Lord (Proverbs 1:7, 9:10) and, for each person, judgment follows death (Hebrews 9:27). For those who have received eternal life through faith in God's gracious provision for salvation in Christ, their eternal destiny is framed by glorious blessing. Those who have rejected this salvation, declaring independence from God through moral rebellion, philosophical speculation, and religious systems, will face eternal consequences that are rooted in God's absolute authority as Creator (Psalm 24:1, 139:1-24; Revelation 20:11-15).

This individual accountability is *consistent* or impartial,[1] always in harmony with God's character and authority, and includes all actions, thoughts, and motives of each person (1 Corinthians 4:1-5). It is *relational* with creatures before the Creator, redeemed servants before the Savior, idolatrous rebels before the holy God at different times and places[2] on *specific* terms, regarding a person's response to God and His revelation (Romans 1:18-3:31). Salvation before God is always rooted in His grace that is provided in Christ's death and experienced only through faith (Ephesians 2:8-9). Religious activities or moral accomplishments are never a basis for forgiveness or a cause for boasting (Galatians 3:6-14; Hebrews 9:11-14, 10:4). Apart from faith in Christ, sinful deeds result in eternal death (Revelation 20:11-

15). Because people are created in God's image for an intimate relationship with Him, these judgments are *eternally significant* for each person—life with Christ or death without Him.

Rewards for Believers is God's Idea

This accountability before God reflects the exhortations of Jesus and Paul for Christ's followers to make eternal investments while on earth. (Matthew 6:19-21; 1 Timothy 6:17-19). These urgent commands to live in ways that result in heavenly treasure confirm a believer's life now will be *significant* in heaven. Repeated statements about faithfulness in small things now leading to faithfulness in large things in heaven (Matthew 19:17, 25:23) occur in parables about the accountability of the steward to the master, leveraging present opportunity for future blessing (Luke 16:1–13).

The Bible speaks clearly about ministry that is pleasing to God: faithfulness as a witness for Christ (Acts 1:8; 2 Corinthians 5:20), especially during suffering (Matthew 5:11-12; Colossians 4:2-6; 1 Peter 3:14-16); spiritual encouragement with believers (Hebrews 6:10, 10:24-25) encouraging maturity and equipping multipliers (Ephesians 4:11-16; 1 Thessalonians 2:4-20; 2 Timothy2:1-7); faithfulness in our vocation (Colossians 3:22-24); generosity with material possessions (Matthew 10:40-42; 2 Corinthians 9:6-11; Philippians 4:15-17); hospitality toward strangers (Luke 14:12-14); wise use of our time (Psalm 90:12; Ephesians 5:15-17); running the race with endurance and looking forward to Christ's return (2 Timothy 4:7-8).[3]

Concern about an emphasis on rewards[4] diminishes the reality every believer in heaven will be conformed to Christ's image (Romans 8:29; Philippians 3:21) and will no longer deal with envy and pride. Ministry motivated by fleshly impulses will be consumed by the fire, and only ministry motivated by gratitude for Christ will remain. There will be no comparison, only celebration with other believers of God's grace in Christ revealed in each person's life.

Both our relationship with God and our partnership with Him in ministry are gifts of grace through faith. We see this in the forgiveness of sin and eternal life provided through Christ's death on the cross (Ephesians 2:8-9). *But our ministry as God's workmanship created in Christ Jesus to do good works prepared by God Himself and empowered by the Holy Spirit is also a work of grace.* Like our salvation in Christ, our service for Him leaves no room for boasting (Ephesians 2:10, 5:18). God receives all the glory for our faithful ministry as we embrace the joy of being joint heirs with Christ (Romans 8:17). There will be no bragging or comparison with others at the Bema Seat and throughout eternity, only humility, gratitude, and great joy as we glorify God for His work through forgiven, often frail, servants who depended on His power to fulfill His purpose.

Judgment for Believers Focuses on Faithfulness and Motivation

The judgment for believers at the heavenly Bema[5] entails a pivotal element of the cleansing of the church as Christ's bride, anticipating an eschatological celebration called the wedding of the Lamb (Revelation 19:7-10).[6] This judgment by Christ for all believers addresses their service as stewards, not their struggles as sinners because He paid for our sin fully on the cross (Hebrews 7:27, 9:12, 9:27-28, 10:1-18). Sin can distract and diminish faithful service and will contribute to the hay, wood, and stubble removed by the fire. The judgment at the Bema Seat refines our ministry so what remains—described as gold, silver, and precious jewels—reveals service shaped by faithfulness, motivated by gratitude toward God (1 Corinthians 4:2-5), and pleasing to Jesus (2 Corinthians 5:9-10). This affirms Jesus's teaching regarding prayer, giving, or fasting done to impress people or manipulate God by providing recognition by people but not a lasting reward from God (Matthew 6:2, 5, 16).

Beginning each day with the awareness that *our choices matter now* becomes pivotal. We can make our choices, but we do not choose our consequences. Paul warned the Galatians that God will not be mocked because each person will reap what he or she sows (Galatians 6:7). The tragic impact of rejecting God's guidance fuels painful relationships, chaotic circumstances, and, for believers, the certainty of God's discipline (Galatians 5:19-21; Hebrews 12:4-11). Solomon stated this reality in positive terms, urging his son to trust the Lord wholeheartedly, following God's wisdom rather than leaning on his own ideas (Proverbs 3:5-6). The blessing of this path includes God smoothing and straightening the journey of life, especially in the hard seasons.

In addition, God's gracious wisdom urges us to make the most of our daily opportunities that are energized by His presence (Ecclesiastes 9:10; Ephesians 5:15). Such a life strengthens relationships (Galatians 5:22-23; Colossians 3:12-25) and multiplies spiritual blessings (John 15:5–11; Philippians 2:1-4). As Paul described intentional multiplication, he reminded Timothy that the farmer receives the first fruits (2 Timothy 2:6). The joy of seeing God at work in our lives and relationships in the present enriches this life (1 Timothy 6:17), giving a momentary taste of the never-ending joy of eternity after finishing our earthly race.

The eternal perspective that makes pleasing Christ at the Bema Seat the central motivation informs a second critical reality: *every day matters forever.* When believers partner with God in His purpose of salvation and blessing, they are laying up treasure in heaven as "a good foundation for the future, so they may take hold of that which is life indeed" (1 Timothy 16:19). This treasure includes service opportunities that reflect faithfulness in the "small things" of this life (Luke 16:10),[7] blessing other believers (1 Thessalonians 2:19-20; Philippians 4:1) and sharing the gospel with people who are not yet believers (Colossians 4:2-6).

The privilege of being used by God and the joy of helping others experience this blessing will shape our heavenly embrace of God's majesty, grace, and goodness. All this will be experienced in an immortal, flawless body with a mind, will and emotions conformed to Christ (Romans 8:39; Philippians 3:21). Every believer will receive affirmation from God (1 Corinthians 4:5).[8] All we have done to faithfully please Christ, even in our frailties on earth, will be enjoyed fully in eternity as we serve God in perfect faithfulness and complete fulfillment. But there is one thing we can do now that we will never do in heaven—tell others how to trust Christ for salvation. Only in this life can we share this amazing message with people who need a Savior—a brief opportunity with eternal significance.

Tangible Crowns and Relational Treasures

This awesome future for every person saved by grace through faith in Christ includes specific crowns mentioned in the Scripture: the crown of life for those who faithfully love Christ (James 1:12; Revelation 2:10), the crown of righteousness for those who long for Christ's appearing (2 Timothy 4:8), the imperishable crown for those who run the race faithfully (1 Corinthians 9:25), and the crown of glory for spiritual leaders who serve humbly with pure motives (1 Peter 5:2-4). These rewards will certainly be cause for joy and worship. But the crowns are tangible symbols of a lasting reality.

When the twenty-four elders lay their crowns before God as an act of worship (Revelation 4:10-11),[9] it seems incomprehensible that any person in heaven will refuse to join in such a glorious, climactic declaration that God alone deserves worship, glory, and honor. Our crowns will remain before God's throne as enduring symbols of our eternal gratitude to God who deserves all the glory.

These significant tangible rewards will affirm that *the most treasured rewards of heaven are relational.* The privilege of intimate fellowship with our Creator and Redeemer will enrich every blessing of being faithful in millennial and heavenly responsibilities and experiencing the spectacular glories of the new heaven and new earth (Revelation 21:1-5, 10-27, 22:1-6). We will be enthralled with the majesty of our God and the greatness of His Son.

As we share in His perfect faithfulness, reflecting His glory, like the moon mirroring the sun's bright light, our triune God remains the source for every dimension of our eternal blessing. God will be the focus of every gaze, the center of every conversation, the source of every delight, and the object of constant worship.

In this spectacular environment, we will share unhindered fellowship with all who are joint heirs with Christ. This joy will be magnified as believers see how God worked His purpose in their lives in the context of relationships. Every conversation in heaven will be joyful, but the experience of joy will be directly connected to the faithfulness and motivation of our ministry to others. Each person's life contains a mixture of motivations that forms a measure of faithfulness, perfectly judged at the Bema Seat by Christ. Any ministry done to impress people or manipulate God will be refined by fire, while faithful service—no matter how small or unnoticed by others—will be rewarded (1 Corinthians 3:5-4:7).

All Full of Joy in Context Shaped by Faithfulness and Motivation

The person, "escaping through the flames," will be full of joy in heaven. Every believer celebrating the blessings of Christ's presence and rejoicing in how God worked (even in the believer's frailty), especially through the faithfulness of others, will embrace the spontaneous celebration of God's amazing grace. Now conformed to Christ's image (Romans 8:29), all believers will experience these blessings without comparison, envy, or arrogance because each will be like Jesus. But the person who humbly pours their life into others in this life, resulting in a multi-generational wave of spiritual fruitfulness, will enjoy this celebration in the context of relationships with believers with whom they joyfully partnered in the gracious work of God.[10]

This relational context that will be enjoyed forever is framed in our daily opportunities of ministry. *Faithful spiritual investments in others, motivated by gratitude to God, shape a believer's capacity to experience joy now and forever.*[11] This explains both the urgency and significance of the exhortation to lay up treasure in heaven. Paul affirmed this concept in personal terms, addressing the Thessalonians as the hope, joy, glory, and crown of exultation when Christ returns (1 Thessalonians 2:19-20). Relationships with the people blessed by God through our lives will be an amazing part of God's reward for us. We will not mingle in a crowd of strangers but in a circle of beloved friends because we will know as we are known (1 Corinthians 13:12).

Among the host of believers in heaven, individuals who nurtured us spiritually and those we helped toward maturity and equipped as multipliers will be a relational treasure, stimulating joy and worship. No envy or arrogance, only joyful celebration of God's greatness and grace will be felt. Intimate, joyful fellowship with other believers will always prompt a grateful, unending celebration of God's goodness. *Rewards are God's idea for His glory and our blessing forever.*

On January 1, 2011, Kathy and I attended the Rose Bowl in sunny Pasadena, California. Having invested seventeen years as the chaplain of the Texas Christian University football team, the week became an amazing experience. After receiving VIP seats at the Rose Parade and enjoying a delicious pregame luncheon, I stood on the sidelines while Kathy sat on the fifth row, watching the game with genuine interest (but through eyes that preferred the University of North Carolina Tar Heels). Though she only knew a handful of the players and coaches, she shared in the excitement when TCU won. She had an after-game field pass and happily made her way to the confetti-filled celebration in a majestic stadium. I watched the game a few feet from the action, hugging players after they made great plays and attempting to be as vocal as possible in my support.

After years with the team, sharing conversations after practices and during road trips, many players and coaches became close friends. A lump swelled in my throat as I watched happy tears flow down the faces of dozens of strong, athletic players and coaches who swarmed the field, celebrating their win over a powerful Wisconsin team. Scout team players jumped with joy on the same sideline. They had on game uniforms and theoretically could have played, but they knew they would not have that blessing although their hard work had been a key factor in a successful season. They invested hundreds of hours in the previous year as part of the team. They enjoyed the special gifts provided at a BCS bowl game and would receive a spectacular ring, declaring them Rose Bowl champions—a distinction they would carry for the rest of their lives.

The team members who played, especially the starting lineup and the star players, had the thrill of impacting the outcome of the game. They expended every ounce of energy and used their intense training to play as a team, accomplishing something none of them expected a few months before. Covered with sweat, and in some cases bloodied by the action, they smiled and cried simultaneously, attempting to absorb the delights of the moment. The coaches, exhausted from months of fifteen-hour days and the stress of preparing for the biggest game of their careers, coupled big smiles with deep sighs. Their faces were marked by exploding grins that were moistened by tears of happiness and relief. None would forget that moment.

Every person on the Rose Bowl turf who wore purple embraced as much joy as they could, each in a different way. Kathy's delight differed from my joy, which did not match the fulfillment of scout team players. And theirs was not as great as the ones who played in the game. Even the backup players experienced a different sense of fulfillment from those in the starting lineups who made decisive plays. For the coaches, it was a career-defining moment—one to be savored all their days.

Unlike championship football teams, God's team is not built on the fastest, strongest, or smartest. There is room for anyone available for the life-changing and eternity-blessing action. Individuals determine whether they are on the field or on the sidelines. God is looking for people He can strengthen "whose heart is completely His" (2 Chronicles 16:9). Engagement in God's work that was prepared for us to bless others will be judged based on faithfulness to the opportunities and grateful motivation to please Christ.

This is a daily privilege that enriches each hour while investing in a joyful eternity far beyond our imaginations (Ephesians 3:20–21).

Christ's followers are *created* to be grateful stewards, *crafted* to joyfully serve Christ, and *certain* to give an account of their stewardship as we enter the glories of salvation in Christ. Make the most of your opportunity (Ephesians 5:15; Colossians 4:5) with confidence that God is always preparing good works (Ephesians 2:10) for believers, depending on His strength with humility and gratitude—for His glory and our blessing.

An Encouraging Thread

Reflect on the people God has used to help weave your life into the tapestry of fruitful ministry. Who are the faithful people you are preparing for fruitful multiplication? God will continue to weave the tapestry. Make the most of your opportunity as a grateful, encouraging thread.

APPENDIX

THE STRUCTURE AND SEQUENCE OF LAUNCHING MULTIPLIERS!

Launching Multipliers! is an intentional path that is designed to prepare people as spiritual multipliers. After decades of discipleship conversations, using materials developed by Cru, Navigators, Search, and other excellent ministries, our ministry developed a discipleship resource that is now available online at no cost. It provides eighteen conversations that are framed by questions and rooted in Scripture, which encourages growth in the privilege of serving God. The methodology reinforces a process that is focused on strategic spiritual multiplication. Since we are created to participate in God's purposes, the truths that are discussed will help a believer experience the blessings of daily fellowship with God. The influence of other discipleship materials is obvious, but the impact of thousands of conversations with stimulating questions and helpful comments cannot be overstated. Questions have been sharpened, added, and, in some cases, deleted as we have learned from our partners.

The structure and sequence of the conversations are shaped by a specific purpose: *Preparing fruitful followers of Christ to equip other faithful multipliers in the distinctive context of one-on-one conversations.* As noted in Chapters 3 to 5, the emphasis on one-on-one meetings is not rooted in a biblical mandate but in the scheduling realities of modern life, the challenge of cultivating genuine trust, and the benefits of a conversation where listening, asking helpful questions, and giving respectful answers are persistently strengthened.

A Consistent Pattern

These discussions build on basic truths about our salvation in Christ. This blessing is embraced through clarity about the believer's enduring identity in Christ and security in a relationship that is anchored in God's faithfulness. A pivotal reality is that, without faith (both in becoming a follower of Christ and daily serving Him), it is impossible to please God. These concepts are frequently mentioned in sermons and other gatherings but not always discussed in ways that emphasize practical obedience.

Each conversation has four sections, beginning with a "What If?" situation that introduces the issue being addressed. The next section is entitled "God Says What?" and includes a key verse to be memorized and discussed in the context of questions (beginning with observation and moving to interpretation) about related biblical passages. The third section is called "So What?" and grapples with these biblical truths in specific ways that affect our lives. The last section is "Now What?" and discusses how both partners pursue specific obedience to the truths discussed.

Our sessions include a dynamic where both partners share insights about specific biblical truths. The purpose is to examine important issues and gain clarity about the perspectives of both partners. Such discussions encourage healthy ways to address honest differences. The "theological connective tissue" within each conversation stimulates faithfulness to the truths of Scripture as well as wisdom for conversations with others who are grappling with these issues.

An Intentional Structure

The *Launching Multipliers!* resource is framed in three sections with each consisting of six conversations. The first is **Established for Growth** and focuses on *foundational* truths for maximizing the *privilege* of being God's servant. These conversations may also function as a follow-up resource for young believers. The sessions reflect the conviction that many Christians seek to serve God with unwitting self-reliance, yielding to anxiety, anger, or arrogance. This approach often focuses on "what we are doing for God" rather than humbly depending on God as we obey. Such intentional dependence is strengthened by confidence in God's Word—anchored by clarity, our spiritual security is assured by God's perfect faithfulness and experienced in harmony with our new identity in Christ. This pattern includes both the structured responsibilities (job, family, ministry) and opportunities unfolding in the context of daily life. These sessions are designed to help new believers with a strong start in personal fellowship with God, as well as encourage mature believers to maximize the blessing of serving Him.

The next six sessions are entitled **Equipped for Ministry** and emphasize a consistent *focus* on biblical *patterns,* guiding progress toward maturity, and enlarging our capacity for spiritual impact. As believers meditate on God's character, they are encouraged to address sin with confession, strengthening both humility before God and gratitude for Christ's sacrificial death. These priorities should be joined with Bible study and the blessing of communicating with God through prayer. As God works in our lives, we enlarge our capacity to address the conflicts that are common in a world of hurting people. This environment of forgiveness and relational blessing enriches our opportunity to invest in multipliers.

The final section, **Empowered for Multiplication**, discusses skills and insights, regarding *perspectives that fuel* an enduring lifestyle of relational evangelism and intentional discipleship. Believers must be prepared to share their spiritual stories, putting the spotlight on Jesus. This priority is energized by confidence in the way God has shaped their lives. It enlarges a believer's capacity to *focus* on fruitful ministry opportunities long-term while being *flexible* to occasionally help with other needs. God's Word teaches that each follower of Christ enjoys the privilege of blessing others while engaging in good works that God has prepared (Ephesians 2:10). A life of spiritual credibility requires wisdom to make decisions, reflecting dependence on God and confidence in His faithfulness even through our mistakes.

A wise follower of Christ embraces the perspective of a steward who will give an account to the Master, Jesus Christ. Stewardship of the assets entrusted to us requires judgment based on faithfulness and motivation (1 Corinthians 4:1–5). Both the soberness of this account-ability and the anticipation of spiritual rewards motivate a pattern of intentional discipleship, preparing others while encouraging a strong finish that honors Christ (Matthew 6:19–21; 1 Timothy 6:17–19; 2 Corinthians 5:9–10; 2 Timothy 4:7-8). The eighteen sessions are designed to help a person obey Paul's exhortation to "hold fast" to sound teaching (2 Timothy 2:13; Titus 1:9) as they guide others through the truths unpacked in *Launching Multipliers!*

THEOLOGICAL INSIGHTS FOR FRUITFUL MULTIPLIERS

During hundreds of discipleship conversations, many of the most helpful insights have been stimulated by a spontaneous question or comment from one of our partners. These insights, anchored in Scripture and framed by God's gracious work in believers, often prompted the exclamation, "Make sure we write this down." Each section connects with one of the eighteen conversations and reflects a decade of fruitful discussions.

Beginning A Christ-Centered Life

- Our creation in the image of the triune God (Genesis 1:26-27; Isaiah 59:19-20) reveals a divine fingerprint: *unity embracing diversity, unleashing creation.* This reality, reflected in marriage and the body of Christ, has profound benefits in a world that is confused about human purpose, marriage, and sexuality.
- Satan continues to use the same strategy in temptation (Genesis 3:1-5; 1 John 2:15-17) because it has been effective with every person except Jesus (Matthew 4:1-11).

- The impulse for sinners to hide from God is universal. God takes the initiative in restoring a person who finds mercy and grace through faith in Christ (Romans 3:26-27; Hebrews 4:12-16; 1 John 1:9). God is the gracious initiator, and believers are grateful responders.
- The rejection of the "bad news" of human sinfulness is prevalent in our world. The biblical teaching of Jesus Christ as Savior for sinful people seems irrelevant to people who minimize sin (Ephesians 2:1-9).
- Sin has sobering consequences. Adam's sin *imputed* to every person (Romans 5:12-17), results in physical death. A sinful nature, *inherited* by every child through the parents (Psalm 51:5; Ephesians 2:3), is revealed in sinful behavior. *Individual* sin includes actions, thoughts, and motives and is the basis for judging all who do not have eternal life in Christ (Revelation 20:11-15).
- People are saved by faith alone. Our works add nothing to what Christ paid on the cross and are never a cause for boasting. The good works that God prepares for believers are empowered by His Spirit for His glory (Matthew 5:16; Ephesians 2:8-10). The message of God's grace requires a personal response of faith in Christ's payment for our sins, validated by Jesus's bodily resurrection. This faith is rational and anchored in the most logical explanation for the empty tomb after Jesus's crucifixion.

Grasping the Faith Process

- The necessity of faith in pleasing God (Hebrews 11:6) is a pivotal truth. Each person has faith in someone or something and worships what is most valued. It is not faith in faith, but faith in God, expressed in obedience to His revealed truth that pleases God (Romans 10:17, 14:23; 2 Corinthians 5:7; Galatians 2:20).

- Faith in what Jesus accomplished on the cross as payment for our sins is how a person begins a relationship with God. Enjoyment of this relationship, described as fellowship with God, is experienced by faith. *Embracing faith* daily results in spiritual stability, fruitful growth, and contagious gratitude (Colossians 2:6-7).
- It is important to *envision obedience* in terms of real-life situations. The starting point is often honesty about nagging areas of disobedience (1 John 1:9). The greater the clarity about disobedience, the more specific the plan for obedience in God's strength.
- The Holy Spirit dwells in each believer (1 Corinthians 12:7). We live by faith as we *expect empowerment* to obey God (Ephesians 1:19, 5:18).
- Both obedience and disobedience impact other areas of life. There is always collateral damage or blessing. Addressing a specific area of obedience will have a broader positive impact, just as continued disobedience poisons other areas.
- We "work out" our salvation as God "works in" us through each step of faith (Philippians 2:12-13).

Building Confidence in God's Word

- God's written revelation has benefits that are psychological, mental, emotional, spiritual, and moral (Psalm 19:7-11). Each time a person is led by the Spirit to embrace the truths of Scripture, these blessings are strengthened.
- Confidence in God's Word is supported by the witness of the Bible (Psalm 119:160; Proverbs 30:5; 2 Peter 1:20-21) and the consistent example of Jesus. The message about God's salvation through Christ was communicated through forty authors in three languages over 1,500 years. No book that claims to be a revelation from God contains

more credible manuscript evidence, broader translation, more extensive distribution, or greater validation by archeological discoveries.

- Fulfilled prophecy stimulates confidence in God's Word. A central focus of prophecy in the Old Testament is the provision of the Messiah for Israel who is the Savior of the world. Examination of these prophecies strengthens confidence in Scripture and anticipation of Christ's promised return (John 14:1-3; 1 Thessalonians 4:13-18).
- The specific benefits of Scripture reflect the circumstances of a believer's life. The same passage can teach, rebuke, correct, and train in righteousness (2 Timothy 3:16-17), depending on a person's spiritual condition.
- Refusal to receive a rebuke and pursue correction leads to God's loving and painful discipline (Hebrews 12:7-11). *Prompt obedience is always the path of wisdom.*

Appreciating Your Security in Christ

- Eternal life begins when a person receives Christ by faith (John 1:12; 1 John 5:11-12) and will never end (John 5:24; 1 John 5:13). This truth, joined with the certainty of the Father's temporal discipline (Hebrews 12:7-11) and ultimate accountability before Christ (Romans 14:12; 2 Corinthians 5:9-10), sharpens a believer's motivation as God's servant.
- Our security as God's adopted child is anchored in the power and faithfulness of the Son and the Father (John 10:28-29). Believers are also sealed until the day of redemption by the Holy Spirit (Ephesians 1:13-14, 4:30). This security is as certain as the power and perfect character of the triune God.
- Nothing, including any part of creation, can separate God's child from His love. Every person who has received

Christ by faith is a created being, so doubt, confusion, or failure will not separate a believer from God (Romans 8:15-17, 38-39).

- The Father's loving discipline of His children (Hebrews 12:7-11) reflects His knowledge of all who belong to Him (2 Timothy 2:19). This discipline is painful and can lead to sickness and even death (1 Corinthians 11:30).
- A believer's judgment by Christ (Romans 14:12; 2 Corinthians 5:9-10) focuses on faithful service and motivates a life that is pleasing to Christ. Our security does not minimize this accountability.
- God's enduring commitment to conform believers to the image of His Son (Romans 8:29) will prevail over the folly of disobedient children.
- Security is related to assurance but must be distinguished from it. Security is established by what God has done for us in Christ, but assurance reflects our understanding of God's faithfulness in completing this gracious work.

Embracing Your Identity in Christ

- Paul declares that God's grace provides freedom from sin's domination, not freedom to continue sinning as believers united with Christ (Romans 6:1-10).
- This new identity is explained in terms of our shared spiritual experience in Christ's crucifixion, burial, and resurrection to live a new life by God's grace through faith. This does not mean we are not capable of sin, but we are no longer obligated to sin.
- Pursuing the patterns that strengthen union with Christ, described as abiding in Him, is a path of blessing. Consistent embrace of this identity glorifies the Father, strengthens our love for Christ, fuels fruitful ministry, guides prayer, and enlarges personal joy (John 15:5-11).

- Our identity as a child of God will be true of us forever and is the basis for a truthful self-perception that helps us maximize the opportunities of this life.
- The *trigger* for experiencing the blessing of being united with Christ is a decisive choice to embrace our new identity in Christ (Romans 6:11).
- The *trajectory* of spiritual transformation is shaped by a daily pattern of presenting our life to God as His instrument (Romans 6:12-23, 12:1-2).
- When people are complacent about sin, they will be mastered by sin. Sin results in divine discipline and destructive temporal consequences for a believer. Prompt confession of sin and restoration of fellowship with God is essential (1 John 1:9).
- It is not surprising that there is a conflict between our fleshly desires and our new identity in Christ. The hope for victory in this battle is found in Christ (Romans 7:15-25) and enjoyed by dependence on God's power (Romans 8:1-39).

Living in God's Presence and Power

- Jesus affirmed the disciples (and all of His followers in the centuries since) have a distinctive advantage with God the Spirit, living within them (John 16:7). Peter declared, "God has granted to us everything pertaining to life and godliness" (2 Peter 1:3).
- There is a daily pattern of encouraging our engagement in God's work (John 5:24). The process of release, respond, and restore has two primary operational outcomes: *dependence mode* or *default mode*.
- Dependence mode is a reliance on God's power to pursue what pleases God. Living in dependence mode requires persistent focus and supernatural help.

- Beginning the day in worship (Romans 12:1–2) helps a believer consciously surrender control to God's Spirit, reflecting a posture of obedience (Romans 6:11-15).
- Looking for ways to be part of what God is doing (Ephesians 2:10) helps a believer see opportunities clearly enough to respond in faith to what God has prepared.
- Default mode requires no intentionality. It is how people normally operate in life from their earliest moments to satisfy selfish desires. This pattern of self-dependence is so prevalent it initially feels normal though it eventually damages relationships and diminishes joy.
- When a person's actions are overtly sinful, there is no confusion about the need to confess our sins; however, the pursuit of what is good does not necessarily mean dependence on God. Ministry that seeks to satisfy self or impress others is sinful and disrupts fellowship with God.
- Indicators that a believer is in default mode include anxiety, anger, and arrogance. Trying harder in the flesh to accomplish God's purposes may impress others or give momentary validation to the person, but the anxiety usually increases. *Anxiety stimulates stress and sabotages joy.*
- Anger is inevitable because it is the human response to hurt. Since we live in a world of hurts, we will get angry, sometimes during ministry opportunities. The question is whether we will remain angry. *Wisely and promptly addressing anger helps people continue in dependence on God* (Ephesians 4:15, 26-32).
- When ministry endeavors have fruitful outcomes, a person doing the ministry can begin to seek applause. *Humility expressed in confession is the consistent remedy for arrogance* (1 Peter 5:6–7).
- Do not delay a fresh start in dependence mode. As we linger before the cross (1 Corinthians 2:2; 1 John 1:7-2:2), resisting a "drive through" mentality, full agreement with

God changes our thoughts about sin and invigorates obedience, reflecting biblical repentance. *Confession is the doorway to repentance, renewing the humility that pleases God and gratitude that motivates fruitful ministry.*

Celebrating God's Character

- The conversation about God's attributes affirms biblical thoughts about God that encourage spiritual wisdom. Each element of God's perfect character strengthens humility before God and confidence in His work in our lives. Three attributes that stimulate vigorous discussion are God's omniscience, immutability, and holiness.
- God's omniscience means He perfectly knows all things, actual and possible, past, present, and future throughout all of eternity (Psalm 139:1-6; Hebrews 4:13). The conversation on how this impacts our prayer life is significant. God's omniscience does not make our prayers less meaningful, because He already knows what He will do. He also knows what we will pray for and incorporates this reality into the outworking of a future fully known to Him. God is faithfully conforming believers into the image of His Son. He tenderly comforts us during life's difficulties and uses our prayers in harmony with His omniscience to fulfill this ultimate purpose.
- God's immutability means His character is unchanging and unchangeable. While He deals with each person uniquely, His attributes in all circumstances remain perfectly consistent (Numbers 23:19; James 1:17). God's response in certain situations is expressed in human terms, suggesting a change of course (Genesis 6; Exodus 32:7-10; Jonah 3:1-10). Since God is eternal and human beings are time-bound, it is not surprising that language struggles to communicate God's unchanging character, engaging with changing human circumstances. Moses, with

gratitude, and Jonah, with exasperation, responded to this tension by affirming God's unchanging faithfulness and love (Exodus 32:11-14; Jonah 4:2). God's work incorporates human choices in ways that are always consistent with His perfect character.

- God's holiness joins His absolute moral *purity* with the ultimate fulfillment of His *purpose.* Our opportunity to obey God's command to "be holy, for I am holy" (Leviticus 11:44–45; 1 Peter 1:15–16) embraces the personal purity that is possible through the obedience that is empowered by the Spirit and the cleansing and forgiveness provided by Christ's sacrifice on the cross. Holiness is not confined to moral issues but includes fulfilling God's purpose in fruitful ministry. Concentrating on both purity and purpose as expressions of God's holiness protects us from unhealthy, legalistic tendencies and centers our lives on the privilege of investing in people with a grateful heart.
- Persistent meditation on God's attributes stimulates worship (Romans 11:33-36), gratitude (Psalm 145:1-21), and a fruitful life (Colossians 1:9-12).

Experiencing God's Forgiveness

- As we linger at the cross, specifically agreeing with God's perspective of our sin, the truth about our problem and God's remedy in Christ changes our perspective on both (Hebrews 10:10). As we focus on God's holiness and love, our lives are transformed by faith expressed in obedience.
- God's forgiveness removes the guilt of our sin (Psalm 103:12; Micah 7:19) and results in cleansing with no condemnation (Romans 8:1; 1 John 1:9).
- This blessing restores our fellowship with God but does not remove the relational consequences of our sin

(Matthew 5:23-26). God gives grace and strength as these issues are addressed and often works in special ways when we seek the forgiveness of others.

- When sin causes a believer to focus inward toward self or outward toward others, a toxic blend of discouragement or arrogance often stunts spiritual growth. Minimizing our sin or marginalizing God's holiness "shrinks" our focus on Christ (1 Corinthians 2:2) and may result in being stuck in default mode. When Christ is our focus, ministry motivated by gratitude enlarges spiritual blessings.
- Feelings of guilt, continuing after genuine confession, indicate a lack of understanding or confidence in the complete sufficiency of Christ's payment for our sin once and for all (Hebrews 7:27, 9:12, 9:27-28, 10:10).

Transformed by God's Word

- Prayer is foundational for fruitful Bible study. The Holy Spirit worked in the lives of the authors of Scripture and dwells in each follower in Christ, guiding toward the truth and yielding fruitfulness (John 14:25-26, 15:26-27; 2 Peter 1:20-21).
- A pattern of inductive Bible study focuses on the value of being doers of the Word and not merely hearers (James 1:22).
- A metaphor, illustrating inductive Bible study, is a mining operation. Observation is digging and sorting the spiritual treasures in a passage. Interpretation examines and determines the significance and relationships of all observations. Application positions this truth for daily expression in our lives.
- The greater the investment in observation of Scripture, the clearer the insights through interpretation and the more practical the personal application.

- A key to fruitful exposition is grasping the immediate *context* of a passage of Scripture as well as its broader *connection* with biblical teaching.
- Knowing and obeying God's Word confirms sound doctrine and healthy living are mutually invigorating (Ezra 7:10; 2 Timothy 1:13-14; Titus 1:9; Hebrews 5:14; James 1:5-7; 1 Peter 2:1-2).
- A concise summary of the key elements of truth in a biblical passage in a single sentence sharpens clarity when teaching God's Word to others.
- God is pleased by faith expressed through obedience to the truths discovered in Scripture (Hebrews 11:6). Hearing God's Word and even deciding to respond, without doing what it says, leads to disorienting spiritual amnesia (James 1:22-24). *Deciding must not be confused with doing.*

Communicating with God

- Prayer is communicating with a perfect Father who engages His children with wisdom and compassion (Psalm 5:1-3, 34:18, 62:5-8; Matthew 7:7-11; James 1:5-7).
- Prayer encourages us to draw near to God with confidence that His faithfulness is always greater than our frailty.
- Jesus is always praying for us (Romans 8:34), and the Holy Spirit prays with us when we do not have a complete understanding of how to pray to the Father (Romans 8:26-27). Since we are never fully aware of all that God desires, the Spirit always prays with us. *We are joining a divine prayer circle each time we pray.*
- Prayer involves four primary dimensions: adoration, confession, thanksgiving, and supplication. Each aspect is important, and prayer does not require a rigid pattern. It is often a spontaneous expression that starts, proceeds, and

concludes differently as we pray, according to the circumstances of life and our intimacy with God.

- Adoration stimulates humility, confession invigorates gratitude, thanksgiving encourages perspective, and supplication strengthens peace.
- As we communicate with God in prayer, the primary means of God's communication with us is the written Scriptures. The Holy Spirit is given to guide and teach us (John 14:25-26, 15:26-27) in harmony with the wisdom found in God's Word (John 16:3) and focused on the Son's glory (John 16:14).
- As we are still and quiet before the Lord (Psalm 46:10, 139:23-24), we may have to "work to listen" in the moment and be "willing to listen" in the hours and days afterward. The Spirit may nudge us toward specific actions that are consistent with Scripture (to pray, encourage, or bless), which we can promptly obey. If the thought is, "Move your family to another city," a more intentional process (discussed in Session 15) is appropriate. In either case, *the Spirit will guide a person who is eager to obey with a mind shaped by Scripture and open to wise counsel.*
- Remember, praying (and giving or fasting) to impress others does not please God and leads only to momentary recognition by people (Matthew 6:1-18).
- God always answers prayer with a "yes," "no," or "not yet." Prayer may be most significant when it leads to spiritual transformation when circumstantial relief is delayed or denied. God does much of His most important work when we are in "the waiting room" of prayer.

Cultivating Healthy Relationships

- Three biblical patterns are foundational for healthy relationships: forgiving, blessing, and pursuing reconciliation with others. These values help God's people shine brightly in dark places (Matthew 5:16; Philippians 2:14-16).

- In a world where hurt is rampant and anger is inevitable, wisely addressing anger is critical. When anger lingers, relationships are damaged and spiritual fruitfulness is compromised (Ephesians 4:29-30).
- Three common anger "languages" are explosion, suppression, and passive aggression. Unresolved anger hurts people and damages relationships Paul challenges believers to reject avoiding the issue or attacking the person by addressing anger honestly and promptly because God has forgiven them in Christ (Ephesians 4:15, 26-32).
- Forgiveness is essential for healthy relationships; God is our model for forgiveness, addressing life's real hurts while making restored relationships possible.
- While forgiveness is a specific step of obedience to God, it is part of a faithful path where a posture of forgiveness is affirmed repeatedly in the emotional and relational dynamics of life. Walking the path of forgiveness is an ongoing aspect of living in dependence mode.
- Forgiveness should not be confused with trust. Forgiveness is given unconditionally because a person has received forgiveness in Christ by grace (Ephesians 4:32). Trust develops in the context of honest communication and behavior (Titus 3:10-11).
- God's Word encourages supportive fellowship with other believers. The "one another" commands of the New Testament (John 13:34-35; 1 John 4:7-10) contribute to healthy relationships (Romans 12:9-12).
- Expressions of tender love are helpful in our relationships, but tough love that confronts the destructiveness of sin is also needed (1 Thessalonians 5:14; Titus 3:10-11).

Enabling behaviors that damage people and relationships
is not loving.
- The urgency for pursuing reconciliation with people we
have harmed prompts an interruption of our worship
(Matthew 5:23–24). This not only strengthens
relationships but often invites opportunities for fruitful
conversations.
- Pursuing reconciliation demonstrates humility before God,
commitment to healthy relationships, and confidence in
His grace in our relationships.

Pursuing Spiritual Multiplication

- Jesus and Paul modeled and commanded intentional
preparation of spiritual multipliers (Luke 6:12-19;
Matthew 28:19-20; 2 Timothy 2:1-7). This focus on
fruitful leaders amplifies the faithfulness of people who
are influenced by larger groups
- One-on-one discipleship is a distinctive form of mentoring
that is aimed at spiritual growth while cultivating
coaching skills that are essential for the strategic purpose
of multiplication (Mark 6-10; Luke 10-11). This
investment in faithful people offers the blessing of both
earthly and eternal rewards (2 Corinthians 5:9-10; 2
Timothy 2:6; 4:7).
- Like all positive mentoring experiences, one-on-one
discipleship is a mutually encouraging relationship that
values a credible example (1 Corinthians 4:16, 11:1) and
consistent humility (Philippians 2:5-11; James 3:13; 1
Peter 5:5-7).
- Credibility is the fruit of character, competence, and
consistency. A believer's wise response to a crisis
amplifies the credibility that is essential in fruitful
discipleship.

- Identifying faithful people requires wisdom (Luke 6:10-19; 2 Timothy 2:2). This process gives a person the opportunity to demonstrate both faithfulness and availability. Paul's description of Timothy (Philippians 2:19-24; 1 Timothy 4:12), Titus (2 Corinthians 8:16-18), and Epaphroditus (Philippians 2:25-30) are instructive for identifying a faithful person.
- Paul describes his investment in the lives of the Thessalonian believers in parenting terms—a mother's nurture and a father's discipline (1 Thessalonians 2:7-12). Tender and tough love wisely expressed strengthens fruitful discipleship.
- When people know they will be discussing discipleship with another person in a few months, they prepare differently, ask questions more carefully, take notes more diligently, and begin praying for their first faithful person in the initial conversation.
- These truths must be absorbed in a context that encourages transparency, accountability, and God-honoring motivations. After months of discussing the truths, developing the skills, and cultivating the attitudes pursued in these sessions, an encouraging, enduring friendship usually will be formed.
- Such relationships are the "first fruits" that are experienced in this life by those who invest in others (2 Timothy 2:6). While the heavenly rewards are greater (1 Thessalonians 2:19-20; 1 Timothy 6:17-19), this appetizer of future blessings is a motivation to continue in serving God by equipping others.

Spotlighting Jesus Through Your Story

- Jesus calls His followers "witnesses" (Acts 1:8), indicating the significance of first-hand knowledge in sharing the message of the gospel with others. What we have experienced personally provides a context for a message that focuses on Christ's payment for our sins (John 5:24).

- This changed life releases the aroma of Christ, a fragrance of life to some, and the stench of death to others (2 Corinthians 2:14-16). While the response to our life and message about Jesus is uncertain, our motivation is compelling—If He died for us, we should live for Him (2 Corinthians 5:14-15).

- With the mindset of an ambassador, we represent Christ in a realm that is hostile to Him and His followers (John 15:18-21) and foreign to us (2 Corinthians 5:20-21). We are faithful in this privilege when we express love even toward adversaries (Romans 12:14-21), following Jesus's example of sharing the hope of eternal life with those who do not yet know the Savior (Mark 2:15-17).

- In this challenging environment, Paul exhorts his readers to demonstrate grace and persuasiveness (Colossians 4:5-6) as they share this message with others.

- A respectful and gentle answer to those who are hostile or curious about our hope in Christ (1 Peter 3:14-16) requires preparation. One way is to develop a summary of your story with a clear explanation of the message of the Gospel. Three elements *form the frame for your story*—your life before trusting Christ, the message you understood when you trusted Christ as Savior, and how knowing Christ has changed your life. Several sentences on that element, presenting a brief, clear explanation of the gospel, will leave a person thinking about Jesus after your story tweaks their interest.

- A personal testimony leverages the reality of our life experience to be a witness and ambassador for our Savior. Whether your story is calm or chaotic, some people will connect when you are honest about your life with gratitude to Christ.

- The concept of a believer's SHAPE emphasizes five aspects of life that affect our fruitful engagement in ministry: Spiritual Gifts, Heart (or passion), Abilities, Personality, and Experiences. Scripture affirms the unique creation of each person (Psalm 139:13-18; Jeremiah 1:4-5) and teaches that a follower of Christ has the privilege of blessing others through good works prepared by God (Ephesians 2:10; 1 Corinthians 12:7).
- Resources that help a person explore spiritual gifts and personality tendencies are available online and at many evangelical churches. Identifying abilities, heart, and experiences can be pursued through personal reflection and honest interaction with close friends about how you best contribute at work, home, or ministry settings.
- Understanding of our distinctive SHAPE requires an availability to serve in ministry to others. This encourages a range of ministry experiences, making an assessment possible. As a believer serves others, God begins to work to increase joy within and the blessing of others. With God's wisdom and the counsel of mature friends, decisions about ministry involvement can be confirmed.
- People who know their SHAPE have the confidence to *focus* on pursuing opportunities where their SHAPE strengthens others. This insight also encourages *flexibility* to respond briefly to urgent needs and the *freedom* to say no to long-term commitments incompatible with a person's SHAPE.

Making Decisions with God's Wisdom

- Knowing and obeying the clear truths of God's Word are the first steps for a life marked by God's grace (James 1:19-22).

- When we disobey God's Word in our daily lives and then ask for wisdom, it leads to being "double-minded." While God may give wisdom mercifully, the capacity to receive it is compromised, resulting in confusion (James 1:5–7).
- God's wisdom helps people discover guidance for important life decisions. This blessing is best experienced when a posture of preemptive obedience is sustained by living in dependence mode.
- As we pray for God's guidance (with our spouse, if married), we allow God to guide our thoughts and conversations. Scripture may provide truth that is directly relevant to a decision. If a decision raises no direct biblical issues, the impact on family or ministry priorities requires consideration since they are always significant.
- A decision needs to be evaluated, considering God's enduring purpose for our lives to glorify Him (Matthew 5:16; 1 Corinthians 10:31-11:1).
- It is important to seek the counsel of mature people (Proverbs 12:15, 15:22, 19:20). This priority is not a shortcut to a wise decision since people often give different perspectives. *Wise counselors help a person ask the right questions so they can move forward with confidence in God's guidance.*
- A final question is appropriate: *What do I desire?* When a person has sought God's wisdom, motivations are often shaped by the "delight in the Lord" during the decision process (Psalm 37:3-4).
- If a decision is made and it becomes obvious that confusion or disobedience led to a poor choice with hard consequences, God will not waste this situation. Some of the wisest counselors gained their most helpful insights from poor decisions.

- Human beings are created by God as stewards of His creation (Genesis 2:15-17), and followers of Christ are stewards of ministry focused on Jesus Christ (1 Peter 4:10).
- As stewards, we are responsible for using tangible, temporal, relational, and spiritual assets that are entrusted to us by God. Our judgment before Christ is based on faithfulness and motivation in using these blessings (1 Corinthians 4:25).
- Wisdom for each aspect of stewardship is revealed in Scripture. Tangible resources require awareness of our vulnerability to greed and the distraction, uncertainty, and brevity inherent in our use of material blessings (Ecclesiastes 5:1-15).
- Temporal assets are a balance of consistency and diversity. Every person receives an equal daily gift of hours, yet no person knows how many days will be given. Each day provides opportunities that matter in the moment and forever (Ecclesiastes 9:10; Ephesians 5:15- 17; 1 Timothy 6:17-19).
- Relational assets are precious because people are made in God's image and will exist for eternity. This stewardship is expressed as we forgive, bless, and pursue reconciliation with others. It shapes our joy and influence in relationships
- Spiritual assets are maximized as we make the most of our SHAPE to encourage and equip believers for ministry to others (1 Corinthians 12:7; Ephesians 4:11-13).
- The judgment of a believer's service and stewardship of God's assets (Romans 14:12; 2 Corinthians 5:9–10) is not focused on sin. Sin has completely been forgiven through Christ's death on the cross. Any emphasis on a believer's

sin at the judgment seat will address sin's impact on faithful service of God.

Sustaining Motivation for Spiritual Multiplication

- Christ's judgment of believers results in rewards for faithful service (Matthew 6:19–21; 1 Corinthians 5:5-15; 1 Timothy 6:17–19). This reality makes each day a gift that matters for eternity during an earthly life that is fleeting like a vapor (James 4:14).
- As stewards, we make our choices, but we do not choose our consequences. God will not be mocked because each person will reap what is sown (Galatians 6:7). The tragic impact of rejecting God's guidance in this life is seen in painful relationships, chaotic consequences, and, for believers, the certainty of God's discipline (Hebrews 12:4–11).
- Obedience to God strengthens relationships (Galatians 5:22–23; Colossians 3:12–25) while enlarging blessings (John 15:5–11; Philippians 2:1–4) and enriching life (1 Timothy 6:17). It is a temporal taste of the joy reserved for us in heaven (1 Timothy 6:19).
- These rewards are associated with crowns in Scripture, including the crown of life (James 1:12; Revelation 2:10), the crown of righteousness (2 Timothy 4:8), the imperishable crown (1 Corinthians 9:25), and the crown of glory (1 Peter 5:2–4). These tangible rewards for specific aspects of faithful ministry will be cause for joyful worship.
- A believer's crowns are symbols of an enduring reality. In fact, when the twenty-four elders lay their crowns before God as an act of worship (Revelation 4:10–11), it seems obvious the throngs in heaven will join in this worship. God deserves all glory and honor for any ministry empowered by His Spirit.

- These tangible rewards will give way to the reality that the *most treasured rewards of heaven are relational.* The privilege of fellowship with our Creator and Redeemer will overwhelm the blessings of being faithful in heavenly responsibilities or experiencing the glories of the new heaven and new earth (Revelation 21:1–5, 10–27, 22:1–6).
- We will share His joy with all who are joint heirs with Christ. This will be magnified as believers see how God worked in our relationships with people. Any ministry done to impress people or manipulate God will be refined by fire while faithful service that is motivated by gratitude to God will be an enduring joy (1 Corinthians 3:10–4:7).
- People saved "escaping through the flames" will be in heaven (1 Corinthians 3:15). There will be no envy, but their joy will be shaped by the spiritual investments of their lives.
- Believers who faithfully serve God will experience heaven's celebrations with the delight of personal participation in God's gracious work. Those they nurtured and equipped will be a relational reward described as a crown and joy (1 Thessalonians 2: 19-20). *Such spiritual investments enlarge our capacity for joy both now and forever.*

Nurturing Spiritual Multipliers

- The Scriptures describe serving Christ as a race. As we fix our eyes on Jesus, *the perfect model of endurance* (Hebrews 12:1-3), we finish strong.
- When we remember God's *salvation in the past,* His pow*er in the present* hardship, and His *glory in the future,* we know it is too soon to lose heart (2 Corinthians 4:1-18).
- Embracing the perspective of the heavenly future prepared

for us helps us steadfastly continue with abundant hope (John 14:1-3; Colossians 3:1-4).

- Faithfulness to individuals and those in group settings is strengthened by a consistent priority on preparing fruitful multipliers.
- Jesus and Paul modeled "constrained availability" (Mark 6:45-52; Luke 9:1-6; 1 Timothy 1:3; Titus 1:5), putting their disciples in situations where they had to depend on God without their mentor being physically present. Trust in God alone ramps up the pace of growth in both faith and skills.
- A consistent example of humility, integrity, and transparency is foundational for launching multipliers. Preparing a spiritually influential person is the purpose, not completing a program. Paul's description of Timothy and Titus emphasized their example of enthusiasm and fruitful ministry (1 Timothy 4:12-16, 6:6-10; Titus 2:7-8).

NOTES

1. WHY ANOTHER BOOK ON DISCIPLESHIP?

1. Michael J. Wilkins, *Following the Master-A Biblical Theology of Discipleship* (Grand Rapids, MI: Zondervan, 1992). Wilkins provides a thorough explanation of the cultural context and biblical nuances related to discipleship.

2. A. B. Bruce, *The Training of the Twelve: Exhibiting the Twelve Disciples Under Discipline for the Apostleship* (New Canaan, CT: Keats Publishing, 1979), 11. Bruce wrote this classic study of Jesus's ministry in 1871. It is foundational for most books on discipleship. Bruce explains the "come and see," "follow me," and "be with me" dimensions of Jesus's ministry.

3. Bill Hull, *The Complete Book of Discipleship* (Colorado Springs, CO: NavPress, 2006). This book focuses on this pivotal aspect of Jesus's pattern of discipleship.

4. Acts 6:1–29:19, 26, 38; 11:26; 13:52; 14:20, 22, 28; 18:23, 27 illustrate this usage.

5. Both our salvation and obedience are possible only by faith through His grace. The cost of obedience, denying yourself and following Christ, is significant and only experienced by intentional dependence on God. The costs of disobedience, including divine discipline, relational damage, and squandered eternal rewards are more sobering. Luke's use of "disciple" in Acts indicates a person in a relationship with Christ by faith rather than a specific affirmation of a person's spiritual vitality in that relationship. Paul's challenging letters to churches in Galatia, Philippi, Thessalonica, and Corinth regarding legalism, fleshly turmoil, relational conflict, rampant anxiety, stubborn laziness, and immorality reveal that believers can struggle with disobedience to God in many ways.

6. An appendix on "The Sequence and Structure of *Launching Multipliers!*" explains the process developed to pursue this priority. Like so many elements of this book, the terms "faithful and focused" surfaced in a discipleship conversation with faithful pastor and fruitful multiplier James Womack.

7. The book of Judges exposes a persistent cycle: spiritual distress, gracious renewal, enthusiastic but short-term obedience, and painful wandering followed by spiritual distress. This pattern unfolded repeatedly for Israel and the church throughout the centuries. More recent revival movements like the First and Second Awakenings in America and England yielded spiritual benefits and prosperity, but, eventually, drifted toward moral decline, political conflict, and frequent wars. In the 1950s, following two global wars, Christianity experienced expanding parachurch ministries, missions organizations, and global revival movements by leaders like Billy Graham. The Jesus Movement in the late 1960s was a dramatic spiritual episode eventually overwhelmed by rampant materialism, immorality, and lingering cultural and spiritual malaise. Spiritual blessings that impact public awareness continue intermittently and may be appreciated and beneficial for a season. History affirms that cultural pressures gradually erode the

integrity of such phenomena (Romans 1 2:1-2), so each new generation must be prepared for a renewed commitment to faithfulness amid intense spiritual hostility. Richard Blackaby wrote about a recent revival episode in Asbury, Kentucky, putting it in a helpful context, emphasizing God's initiative, individual repentance, the prominent role of God's Word, the possibility of genuine spiritual blessings, and what he sees as the eventual end of revival movements. ("Reflections on Revival," www.richardblackaby.com, February 15, 2023).

2. EXAMINING BIBLICAL EXAMPLES AND EXHORTATIONS FOR EQUIPPING DISCIPLES

1. Robert Coleman, *The Master Plan of Evangelism* (Grand Rapids, MI: Revell, 1998). Originally published in 1963, this book makes a pivotal contribution to the discussion of discipleship. Coleman describes this strategy when he writes, "His concern was not with programs to reach multitudes, but with men whom the multitudes would follow" (p. 21). Paul makes it clear that men and women are privileged to be part of this strategic purpose (Titus 2:1-8).
2. Ibid., 21.
3. A second imperative translated "Lo" or "Behold" is used in verse 20 to make this final point more emphatic.
4. John McRay, *PAUL: His Life and Teaching* (Grand Rapids, MI: Baker Academic, 2003), 25-26. Saul was his Jewish name and Paul his Roman name. He would have received those names in childhood and used the name appropriate for the situation. Saul as a former Jewish Pharisee in his early ministry, and Paul as a Roman citizen called to "preach among the Gentiles" (Galatians 1:16).
5. Jason Byassee, "Who was Henrietta Mears?" Christian Century, March 30, 2021.
6. Henrietta Mears, *What the Bible Is All About* (Ventura, CA: Gospel Light Publications, 1983).
7. Earl O. Roe, Editor, *Dream Big: The Henrietta Mears Story* (Ventura, CA: Regal Books, 1990), 323.
8. Matt Brown, "The Hundred Year Influence of Henrietta Mears," thinke, August 1, 2018, www. thinke.org/blog/henrietta-mears.
9. Jason Byassee, "Who Was Henrietta Mears?", The Christian Century, April 7, 2021, www. www.christiancentury.org/review/books/who-was-henrietta-mears.
10. Arlin C. Migliazzo, "Without Henrietta Mears, Evangelicalism as We Know It Probably Wouldn't Exist," Christianity Today, March 11, 2021, www.christianitytoday.com/ct/2021/march-web-only/henrietta-mears-mother-evangelicalism-arlin-migliazzo.html.
11. Earl O. Roe, *Dream Big: The Henrietta Mears Story* (Carol Stream, IL: Tyndale House Publishers, June 7, 2016).
12. George Marsden, "The Mother of Modern Evangelicalism, Review: The Mother of Modern Evangelism: The Life and Legacy of Henrietta Mears," The Gospel Coalition, January 25, 2021. www.thegospelcoalition.org/reviews/mother-evangelicalism-henrietta-mears/.
13. Arlin C. Migliazzo, "Without Henrietta Mears, Evangelicalism as We Know It Probably Wouldn't Exist," Christianity Today, March 11, 2021, www.christianity-

today.com/ct/2021/march-web-only/henrietta-mears-mother-evangelicalism-arlin-migliazzo.html.

3. FOUNDATIONAL VALUES FOR FRUITFUL MULTIPLIERS

1. This inevitability of humility reflects Paul's declaration "every knee will bow" before Christ (Philippians 2:10). Whether through grateful faith in Christ in this life or under sovereign compulsion at the final judgment of all who rejected God's grace, the reality of Christ's Lordship over all will be acknowledged.

2. Jon Sherman, "The Habits of Jesus: A Spiritual Weapon," Trinity Bible Church, October 2, 2022. www. trinitybible.com/sermons/the-habits-of-jesus-scripture/. Sherman brings these various elements into sharp focus. A suggested method for memorization might help: SEE/HEAR/SAY/WRITE/REPEAT.

3. Jim Putman, *Real Life Discipleship: Building Churches That Make Disciples* (Colorado Springs, CO: NavPress, 2010); Jim Putnam, Avery T. Willis, Jr. Brandon Guindon and Bill Krause, *Real Life Discipleship Training Manual* (Colorado Springs, CO: NavPress, 2010).

4. Chris Swain and Robbie Gallaty, *Replicate: How to Create a Culture of Disciple-Making Right Where You Are* (Chicago: Moody Publishers, 2020).

5. Ibid.

6. Over fifty commands like "love one another" (John 13:34), "encourage one another" (Hebrews 13:3), "admonish one another" (Romans 15:14) impact individual relationships in all settings. This important aspect of fruitful living is explained in Chapter 8.

7. Greg Ogden, *Transforming Discipleship: Making Disciples a Few at a Time* (Colorado Springs, CO: IVP Books, 2003), 140-48.

8. Ibid., 154–69.

9. *Launching Multipliers!* is an eighteen-session conversation aimed at preparing intentional multipliers for fruitful influence in their churches, families, neighborhoods, and other spheres of influence. Many churches have made this process a central aspect of their leadership development process. It is available for personal and local church use and can be downloaded at www.ministrycatalysts.com in numerous languages. You may also adapt this resource to the needs of your ministry. Other books offering a pattern for one-on-one or group discipleship include the following: Mark Bailey, *To Follow Him: The Seven Marks of a Disciple* (Sisters, OR: Multnomah, 1997); Francis Chan and David Platt, *Multiply: Disciples Making Disciples* (Colorado Springs: David C. Cook, 2012); Stacy T. Rinehart, *Lead in the Light of Eternity: The Jesus Model* (Colorado Springs, CO: MentorLink International, 2015); John Tolson and Larry Kreider, *The Four Priorities: Life's Too Short to Get It Wrong* (Dallas, TX: High Impact Life, 2012).

10. All dates about the history of the church are A.D. and will not be noted.

11. *Eerdmans' Handbook to the History of Christianity: "John and Charles Wesley"* Tim Dowley, Editor (Hertz, England: Lion Publishing, 1977), 447. This group known as the Holy Club included his brother, Charles, and George Whitfield.

12. Bruce L. Shelley, *Church History in Plain Language, Updated 2nd Edition* (Nashville: Thomas Nelson Publishers, 1995), 33.

13. John D. Hannah, *Invitation to Church History: World* (Grand Rapids, MI: Kregel Publishers, 2018), 418.
14. Laurence Wood, *Pentecost & Sanctification in the Writings of John Wesley and Charles Wesley With a Proposal for Today* (Jackson, GA: Emeth Press, April 24, 2018), 448.
15. Bruce L. Shelley, *Church History in Plain Language, Updated 2nd Edition* (Nashville: Thomas Nelson Publishers, 1995), 339. Wesley followed the Moravian group model.
16. "Wesley to Wilberforce," Church History Institute. www. christianhistoryinstitute.org/magazine/article/wesley-to-wilberforce.

4. ESSENTIAL SKILLS FOR FRUITFUL MULTIPLIERS

1. J. Arthur Smith, *The Master Coach Model* (High Point, NC: Leadership Systems, Inc., 2015). This is a delineation of a two-day seminar for business leaders from a broad range of industries. Participating in the seminar fueled my capacity to respond to the wise counsel of my older friend.
2. LeadingWithQuestions.com is an excellent resource. This website incorporates Bob Tiede's valuable insights but also highlights information from other contributors in this important area. Books with helpful perspectives include the following: Gary R. Collins, *Christian Coaching: Helping Others Turn Potential into Reality* (Colorado Springs, CO: NavPress, 2009); and Tony Stoltzfus, *Leadership Coaching: The Disciplines, Skills and Heart of a Christian Coach* (Charleston, SC: BookSurge Publishing, 2005).
3. World of Work, "Mehrabian's 7-38-55 Communication Model: It's More Than Words," www.worldofwork.io/2019/07.
4. J. Arthur Smith, *The Master Coach Model* (High Point, NC: Leadership Systems, Inc., 2015). 39–67. This book focuses on using questions in the coaching process and illustrates this principle with experiences in athletics, business, professional skills, nature, and practical examples.
5. Jesus illustrates this pattern in many settings. See Matthew 7:24–27 (building a house on sand or rock) and Luke 15 (losing and finding a sheep, a coin, or a son).
6. *Eerdmans' Handbook to the History of Christianity: "Justin Martyr"* Tim Dowley, Editor (Hertz, England: Lion Publishing, 1977), 108.
7. John D. Hannah, *Invitation To Church History: World* (Grand Rapids, MI: Kregel Academy, January 26, 2019), 80-82.
8. *Eerdmans' Handbook to the History of Christianity: "Justin Martyr"* Tim Dowley, Editor (Hertz, England: Lion Publishing, 1977), 108.

5. A PARADIGM FOR HONEST, RESPECTFUL CONVERSATIONS

1. Jude 3–4 commands a vigorous defense of our faith in Christ. Jesus (John 3:1–4) and Paul (Acts 17:22–34, 26:2–29) demonstrate consistency with this principle in an intentionally persuasive model marked by gentleness and respect (1 Peter 3:15).

2. James Arthur Smith, "An Intentional Use of Questions as a Basis for Educational Feedback," (D.Min. dissertation, Dallas Theological Seminary, 1998), 22. A chart at the end of his dissertation links each question to one of six categories. These insights are adapted as a coaching model in Arthur Smith's book, The Master Coach Model.

3. Classic apologetic resources include *Mere Christianity* by C.S. Lewis as well as *More than a Carpenter* and *Evidence that Demands a Verdict* by Josh McDowell. More recent authors like Lee Strobel, *The Case for Christ* (Grand Rapids, MI: Zondervan, 1998); Tim Keller, *The Reason for God: Belief in the Age of Skepticism* (New York: Riverhead Books, 2008), and John Hopper, *Questioning God* (Fort Worth, TX: Search Ministries, 2021) grapple with a reasoned defense of the biblical message of salvation experienced through faith in Christ.

4. Search Ministries (www.searchnational.org) has online podcasts and other resources focused on discussing these issues with skeptical listeners. One particularly helpful resource focuses on conversations about the most common questions asked by skeptical people. It is available at www.thesearchformeaning.org.

5. Knowing what and where the Bible speaks on the issues under discussion in our culture is a critical element for fruitful conversations. Intentional multiplication focuses on careful inductive study and obedience to Scripture.

6. COMMUNICATING HISTORY'S MOST AMAZING MESSAGE

1. The judgment seat of Christ also known as the bema seat. www.gotquestions.org/judgment-seat-Christ.html.

2. Acts 16:31. Paul and Silas communicated the reality of the message through their worship (after receiving a beating) and their focus on the well-being of the jailer. They answer his query about how to be saved with, "Believe on the Lord Jesus and you will be saved."

3. The Greek word *freely* (or *as a gift*) in Romans 3:24 is translated *without a cause* in John 15:25 in the context of Jesus experiencing hatred. A believer does nothing to earn salvation.

4. Anselm (1033-1109), the archbishop of Canterbury after the Norman conquest of England wrote *Why the God-Man?* It became an enduring contribution to sound doctrine by demonstrating the rational coherency of the biblical revelation of this profound truth.

John D. Hannah, *Invitation to Church History: World* (Grand Rapids, MI: Kregel Publishers, 2018), 232.

5. Dallas Theological Seminary Doctrinal Statement, Article VII. Many books have been written about the nuances communicated in this statement. Prominent books including John F. MacArthur Jr., *The Gospel According to Jesus: What Is Authentic Faith?* (Grand Rapids, MI: Zondervan, 1988) and Zane Hodges, *Absolutely Free: A Biblical Reply to Lordship Salvation* (Redención Viva, 1989) fueled a debate on the biblical message of the gospel during the late 1980s. Charles Swindoll, *The Grace Awakening* (Nashville: Thomas Nelson, 2003) and Charles Ryrie,*So Great A Salvation* (Chicago: Moody Press, 1989) have addressed these debated issues with theological clarity and practical wisdom. Swindoll provides a

biblical exposition of grace, which addresses this controversy without mentioning MacArthur. Ryrie focuses on the critical importance of clear definitions (Charles Ryrie, *So Great Salvation* (Chicago, IL: Moody, July 1, 1997), pp. 21–24) as he addresses the "straw men" he perceives in much of the debate (pp. 27–33). Darrell L. Bock, ("A Review of The Gospel According to Jesus," Galaxy Software Electronic Publishing, (January 1989), www.galaxie.com/article/bsac146-581-03.) has a brief but helpful review. Bock illustrates MacArthur's tendency to make absolute statements in the text with moderating comments in the footnotes and seeks to clarify some of MacArthur's views (pp. 22-25). MacArthur sees real issues like the possibility of false profession of faith in Christ and communicating the gospel without clearly connecting the bad news of our sinfulness with the good news of Christ's payment sin (pp. 25-26). His remedy emphasizes a person's understanding and awareness of Christ's lordship as the Gospel is received. MacArthur's view unfortunately provokes doubt and distracts from the truths of security and discipline rooted in God's faithfulness.

6. John Hopper, *Questioning God? Answers to Questions Worth Asking* (Oklahoma City, OK: Search Ministries, 2021), 167-76, outlines a concise explanation of this crucial issue.

7. Dietrich Bonhoeffer, *The Cost of Discipleship* (New York: Touchtone, 1959), 43-44. In a book originally written in 1937, Bonhoeffer focuses on the Gospel and its implications in the context of tyrannical fascism and liturgical German Lutheranism between the two World Wars. It is a powerful, penetrating, and prophetic, grappling with the gospel message and obedience pleasing to God.

8. 1 Corinthians 3:1-3, 6:1-20; Ephesians 4:28-31, 5:3-14; James 3:5-10, 4:1-5; 1 John 1:8-2:2. These passages illustrate a pattern found in most letters. James's letter does not undermine the "faith alone" uniqueness of the gospel. It does emphasize the reality we begin by faith and are called to live by faith (Galatians 5:16-26) in ways bearing fruit, blessing others, and honoring God. When this pattern is not discernible, James challenges his readers, presumed to be believers, to deal with the issue with humility and obedience (James 4:7-10). For the disobedient believer, God's discipline may be compelling evidence of faith at work in a believer's life. This experience is described in tumultuous, personal terms.

9. *Eerdmans' Handbook to the History of Christianity: "Athanasius"* Everett Ferguson, (Hertz, England: Lion Publishing, 1977), 136.

10. *Eerdmans' Handbook to the History of Christianity: "Ambrose of Milan"* Michael A. Smith, (Hertz, England: Lion Publishing, 1977), 140.

11. Bruce L. Shelley, *Church History in Plain Language, Updated 2nd Edition* (Nashville: Thomas Nelson Publishers, 1995), 97-98.

12. Ibid., 125-131.

13. John D. Hannah, *Invitation to Church History: World* (Grand Rapids, MI: Kregel Publishers, 2018), 134-141.

14. Bruce L. Shelley, *Church History in Plain Language, Updated 2nd Edition* (Nashville: Thomas Nelson Publishers, 1995), 200-203.

15. John D. Hannah, *Invitation to Church History: World* (Grand Rapids, MI: Kregel Publishers, 2018), 314.

7. EMBRACING LIFE'S MOST AWESOME PRIVILEGE

1. I wrote the date in my Bible during his teaching.
2. The word translated *count* is an accounting term associated with credits and debits.
3. John Owen, *The Mortification of Sin: A Puritan View of How to Deal with Sin in Your Life* (Fearne, Tain, Ross-shire, Scotland: Christian focus Publications, Ltd. 1996). He wrote a classic treatment of these issues; his pastoral and theological insights emphasize the persistent pressure of the sinful flesh in a believer's life (pp. 6-7), the destructive impact of sinful choices in a believer's relationships (pp. 9-13), and the necessity and sufficiency of the Spirit's power to deal with these sinful impulses (pp. 14-16) as a believer experiences God's grace that flourishes through intimate, obedient fellowship and fruitful ministry (pp. 17-19).
4. This definition in Session 2 of *Launching Multipliers!* is an anchor point for discussions on living in dependence on God. This section amplifies insights on the faith process developed by Ron and Belle Proctor, *Mentoring 101: Book 1* (Life Builders, 2008), 8. There is a powerful book that addresses the privileges of the Christian life explained through the numerous letters written by John Newton, a former slave trader, long-time pastor, and author of "Amazing Grace" (Tony Reinke, *Newton on the Christian Life* (Wheaton, IL: Crossway, 2015)). Newton's sermons and theological writings were not widely distributed, but he wrote hundreds of letters to acquaintances who were seeking his counsel. This book is a blend of biblical teaching, theological perspective, and encouraging wisdom, explaining the joy and blessings of a Christian life in harmony with Paul's declaration, "to live is Christ" (Philippians 1:21). Newton summarizes his perspective as simplicity of intention joined with "simplicity of dependence leading to genuine obedience" (p. 104), yielding joy even in the distressing circumstances of life (pp. 87-89).
5. Righteous anger at sin is not an indicator of default mode; however, what begins as hatred of sin can quickly become hostility toward the people involved. In that case, unresolved anger will have destructive consequences.
6. These three are foundational to patience, kindness, goodness, faithfulness, gentleness, and self-control listed in Galatians 5:22–23.
7. *Eerdmans' Handbook to the History of Christianity: "Patrick"* Robert G. Clouse, (Hertz, England: Lion Publishing, 1977), 211.
8. Ibid., 212.
9. John D. Hannah, *Invitation to Church History: World* (Grand Rapids, MI: Kregel Publishers, 2018), 177-178.
10. Thomas Cahill, *How the Irish Saved Civilization* (New York: Anchor Books, 1995).

8. CULTIVATING PATTERNS OF FAITHFUL MINISTRY

1. Les Carter, *The Anger Trap: Free Yourself from the Frustrations That Sabotage Your Life* (San Francisco: Jossey-Bass, 2003). This book offers keen insights into

the patterns and consequences of anger as well as a healthy pattern for addressing anger.

2. Andrew Mason, "The 59 One Anothers of the Bible," Small Group Churches, www.smallgroupchurches.com/the-59-one-anothers-of-the-bible/.

3. Ephesians 4:11–12. This passage mentions apostles, prophets, evangelists, pastors, and teachers who equip believers for fruitful ministry.

4. Steve Bateman, *Brothers, Stand Firm: 7 Things Every Man Should Know, Practice, and Invest in the Next Generation* (Eugene, OR: Wipf & Stock, 2014), 17–21.

5. Scott Berkun, "How the Post-It Note Was Invented," Scott Berkun, February 16, 2017, www.scottberkun.com/2017/how-the-post-it-note-was-invented/.

6. Bill Thrasher, *How to Resurrect a Dead Prayer Life* (Chicago: Moody Publishers, 2023). Bill has taught on theology, the spiritual life, and discipleship at Moody Bible Institute since 1980. A brief, helpful encouragement for fruitful prayer can be found in his book.

7. 2 Corinthians 4:1–18. This passage sees the past (mercy), present (power), and future (glory) through the lens of God's unchanging character. Thankfulness frames Paul's exhortation regarding prayer during anxiety (Philippians 4:6–7).

8. Five simple diagrams explained in Session 1 of *Launching Multipliers!* illustrate this approach.

9. Bruce L. Shelley, *Church History in Plain Language, Updated 2nd Edition* (Nashville: Thomas Nelson Publishers, 1995), 208.

10. John D. Hannah, *Invitation to Church History: World* (Grand Rapids, MI: Kregel Publishers, 2018), 257. The Catholic Church excommunicated Waldo's followers at the Council of Verona (1184).

11. *Eerdmans' Handbook to the History of Christianity: "John Wyclif"* Tim Dowley, Editor (Hertz, England: Lion Publishing, 1977), 338.

12. Bruce L. Shelley, *Church History in Plain Language, Updated 2nd Edition* (Nashville: Thomas Nelson Publishers, 1995), 226.

13. Ibid., 231-232.

14. Roger E. Olson, *The Story of Christian Theology: Twenty Centuries of Tradition and Reform* (Downers Grove, IL: InterVarsity Press, 1990), 360–61.

15. Ibid., 370–71. Originally, the Reformers affirmed three solas: Scripture, grace, and faith. Later, theologians sought to clarify Reformed theology by adding "by Christ alone" and "for God's glory alone."

16. Anabaptists and non-conforming churches had influence but less impact on the political affairs of European nations in the centuries following the Reformation.

17. Roland Allen, *The Spontaneous Expansion of the Church: And the Causes Which Hinder It* (Grand Rapids: Wm. B. Eerdmans Publishing Co., 1962). This book, first published in 1927 and authored by a British missionary to China, demonstrated through an examination of Paul's ministry the spiritual and relational empowerment of indigenous believers as a defining factor in missionary expansion. Bureaucracy designed by distant organizational leaders hindered this supernatural dynamic.

18. John D. Hannah, *Invitation to Church History: World* (Grand Rapids, MI: Kregel Publishers, 2018), 308.

19. Bruce L. Shelley, *Church History in Plain Language, Updated 2nd Edition* (Nashville: Thomas Nelson Publishers, 1995), 33. Zwingli, the great Reformer in

Zurich, affirmed the town council's decision to execute some of his disciples who decided that adult baptism was the biblical pattern.

John D. Hannah, *Invitation to Church History: World* (Grand Rapids, MI: Kregel Publishers, 2018), 309. He had a strong disagreement with Luther about the Lord's supper and later died in a military conflict with the Catholic forces in 1531.

20. *Eerdmans' Handbook to the History of Christianity: "John Bunyan"* Tim Dowley, Editor (Hertz, England: Lion Publishing, 1977), 392-393. In the late sixteenth Century, France endured the Huguenot Wars; Germany was devastated by the Thirty Years War (1618–48). England was repeatedly convulsed by wars between the armies of Catholic, Anglican, and Puritan leaders through much of the 17th Century. Even in this chaos, leaders like John Bunyan wrote Pilgrim's Progress portraying the values of pietism.

9. ENLARGING THE JOY OF MULTIPLICATION

1. Judas was an obvious exception.
2. The acronym FAITH described in this paragraph reflects an adaptation of FAT (Faithful, Available, Teachable), which has been in circulation for decades. Following Jesus in prayer for possible, preparing, and practicing multipliers is foundational in identifying and investing in faithful people.
3. God uses women in strategic ministry in many settings. Lydia in Philippi (Acts 16:14, 40), Priscilla (Acts 18:26), Phoebe in Rome (Romans 16:1), and Euodia and Syntyche in Philippi (Philippians 4:2-4) illustrate this in the early church. The amazing impact of Henrietta Mears in the last century was briefly described in Chapter 2. She focused her teaching on children and students by providing a compelling example of strategic motivation for numerous young leaders, including many men, in her extensive ministry.
4. Charles Ryrie, *A Survey of Bible Doctrine* (Chicago: Moody Publishers, 1972). This book has helped strengthen multipliers with a distinctive blend of clarity, thoroughness, and simplicity on theological issues.
5. Kate Shellnutt, "The Pastors Aren't All Right: 38% Consider Leaving Ministry," Christianity Today, November 16, 2021.
6. Bruce L. Shelley, *Church History in Plain Language, Updated 2nd Edition* (Nashville: Thomas Nelson Publishers, 1995), 326-328.
7. Ibid., 375. An Inquiry into the Obligation of Christians to Use Means for the Conversion of the Heathens was published in 1792.
8. *Eerdmans' Handbook to the History of Christianity: "William Carey"* D.W. Bebbington, (Hertz, England: Lion Publishing, 1977), 548.
9. Bruce L. Shelley, *Church History in Plain Language, Updated 2nd Edition* (Nashville: Thomas Nelson Publishers, 1995), 375.
10. Ibid., 376.

10. ANTICIPATING ETERNAL REWARDS

1. Mark Hitchcock, *Heavenly Rewards* (Eugene, OR: Harvest House Publishers, 2019), 31. Hitchcock describes rewards as "earned" because of 1 Corinthians 3:8

where a believer's labor is rewarded. Elsewhere, he affirms that rewards are individual and impartial (pp. 40-47) and that any reward received is due to God's grace (p. 67).

2. Jesus Christ judges His body—the church—at the heavenly Bema Seat (2 Corinthians 5:9–10) and as the millennial King will exercise His divine authority. The judge on the Great White Throne is described as the one "from whose presence heaven and earth fled away" (Revelation 20:11). The other judgments either mention God or are in a context where divine authority is clearly being exercised. These judgments include both deceased and living Jews at the time of their eschatological, national rescue (Daniel 12:1–3; Ezekial 20:33–38; Zechariah 12:10), judgment of those who are martyred for their faithfulness to Christ during the Tribulation (Revelation 20:4–6), and judgment of Gentiles who survive the eschatological tribulation and enter the Millennium (Joel 3:1–2; Matthew 25:31–46).

3. Mark Hitchcock, *Heavenly Rewards* (Eugene, OR: Harvest House Publishers, 2019), 108-123. Hitchcock provides a helpful theological survey on eternal rewards.

4. Craig L. Blomberg, "Degrees of Reward in the Kingdom of Heaven," JETS 35/2 (June 1992), etsjets.org/wp-content/uploads/2010/07/files_JETS-PDFs_35_35-2_JETS_35-2_159-172_Blomberg.pdf. Blomberg rejects an emphasis on distinctive heavenly rewards because of comparison and competition in this life and a perceived hierarchy in eternity. He also assumes distinctive rewards reflect merit (pp.164-169). Ministry motivated by fleshly impulses now will be consumed by the fire and only ministry motivated by gratitude for Christ will remain. Our relationships with other believers will forever frame our celebration focused on God's gracious work.

5. The Bema Seat adjacent to the city of Corinth still exists and was the place of both judicial pronouncement and the award of crowns made of entwined plants given to winners of the athletic games nearby.

6. The marriage of Christ and the Church (Ephesians 5:22-33) suggests a distinctive cultural context for eschatological events. After the believers in Christ, living at the moment of promised deliverance, are joined in the air with those who have died since Pentecost, the Lord Jesus will return to heaven with His bride—the church. In the place He has prepared (John 14:6), a judgment of people who are in Christ's body will occur after the living believers are joined with those believers who have already died (1 Thessalonians 4:13–18). Known as the Rapture (rooted in the Latin rapture, translating the Greek word meaning snatching up), the timing of this event is debated in various eschatological perspectives, but the certainty of it remains essential in Paul's encouragement for the Thessalonians. The church as Christ's bride will be purified in anticipation of a heavenly wedding with the bride clothed in white linen, signifying purity and righteous acts (Revelation 19:7–10). It will be followed by a triumphant return to earth followed by a thousand years (Revelation 20:4-6) of political peace (Isaiah 11:6-9, 19:23-25), material prosperity (Isaiah 35:1-10, 60:1-22) and spiritual vitality (Isaiah 2:2-4, 61:1-11).

Charles C. Ryrie, *Come Quickly, Lord Jesus* (Eugene, OR: Harvest House Publishers, 1996), 67.

This event will be a global wedding banquet worthy of the King of kings and His bride. The connections between this prophesied future and the Jewish cultural patterns for marriage are striking: a price was paid for the bride prior to the process; a bridal chamber was built by the groom at his father's home before the wedding; the groom escorted his bride to this new home. The Millennium under Christ's rule on earth is the wedding banquet, and eternity in the new heaven and new earth will be our forever home.

7. The apostles will sit on thrones over the twelve tribes of Israel (Matthew 19:28); saints will judge the world with Christ (1 Corinthians 6:2); David will serve with the Messiah as the prince over Israel (Ezekial 37:24–26); and those martyred during the Tribulation will reign with Christ during the Millennium (Revelation 20:4). While there is debate about the timing of these experiences, the future of God's redeemed will involve service connected to faithfulness in this life.

8. Mark Hitchcock, *Heavenly Rewards* (Eugene, OR: Harvest House Publishers, 2019), 66-67. Though the way God uses each person may not be obvious to others, God knows every thought and motive.

9. The identity of this group (Revelation 4:4, 10, 5:8, 19:4) is debated, with views from angels to church leaders or leaders of Israel and the church. Being dressed in white and wearing crowns suggests church leaders initiating this heavenly worship.

10. Craig L. Blomberg, "Degrees of Reward in the Kingdom of Heaven," JETS 35/2 (June 1992), etsjets.org/wp-content/uploads/2010/07/files_JETS-PDFs_35_35-2_JETS_35-2_159-172_Blomberg.pdf. Blomberg vigorously opposes distinctions between believers regarding rewards. Issues like regret, envy, or proud displays are noted; however, he states, "All true believers will experience some such exaltation, no doubt in varying ways," even as he opposes differences based on crowns. This is close to the view proposed in this chapter. Every believer will be full of joy, each with a personal capacity, reflecting the treasures laid up in heaven through relational investments rooted in humility before God and gratitude for Christ.

11. Mark Hitchcock, *Heavenly Rewards* (Eugene, OR: Harvest House Publishers, 2019), 88. Hitchcock uses this concept of "capacity" regarding a believer's experience in heaven. His emphasis is on the capacity to glorify God. Our resource developed over a decade ago emphasizes our capacity to experience joy in God's presence. My view is that believers reflect God's glory—just as the moon reflects the sun's light—as they enjoy the blessings of being joint heirs with Jesus. The agreement is more significant than the different emphases.

ABOUT THE AUTHOR

Dr. Ken Horton was raised in a Christian home where he trusted Christ as a young boy, took his first steps spiritually in a growing church, was exposed to intentional discipleship through Cru at Auburn University, and began a decades long learning experience in this great privilege of service to the Lord, while serving as a Space Surveillance Officer in the Air Force. Ken's growing passion to equip faithful believers as strategic multipliers has been fueled by many things: the blessings of family alongside his wife, Kathy, and their children, enjoying a long, fruitful pastorate in Texas, completing a PhD in historical theology, serving two decades as the chaplain for the Texas Christian University football team, and teaching global missions partners for many years.